S0-ACW-999

THE ROYALS

THEIR LIVES, LOVES AND SECRETS

CONTENTS

THE ROYALS

For all their wealth and power, the world's remaining royal families are relics of another age. Living in a world where celebrating Grandma's birthday means having a parade and inviting the entire country, the Windsors will forever represent the glory days of the British Empire. The Grimaldis, ensconced in a pink palace where Grace Kelly came to live as a bride, are reminders of her once-upon-a-time love affair with Monaco's Prince Rainier. And in Japan, Emperor Akihito's dynasty were once believed to be descended from gods. In reality, members of these regal clans are all too mortal: Witness all the riveting human drama that goes on behind the pageantry and pomp. Throw in decades of extravagant weddings (Spain's Prince Felipe and Letizia Ortiz), ignominious divorces (Queen Elizabeth's brood) and irresistible scandals (Prince Albert's illegitimate children), and you have a beat that has

heir lives, loves and secrets

yielded some of the most memorable stories in PEOPLE's 32-year history.

In all that reporting, there is a constant thread: To be royal is to live a life of incredible privilege. But it also means dwelling under a microscope, where missteps become headlines. Members of a royal house learn early that they are bound by duty and tradition; those who marry into the fold can find it hard to adapt. Outsiders who diss the in-laws (Diana) or spend like a Trump (Fergie) are often ostracized by the royal inner circle for tarnishing the crown.

Despite all their perks, it's not hard to empathize with those whose personal flaws can become matters of state. Even today, failed attempts to produce an heir can end dynasties, a bad marriage can divide a kingdom, and a tragedy, such as Diana's 1997 death, can rock the realm.

PEOPLE's first royal cover, on Nov. 11, 1974, featured Prince Charles: "He's Turning 26 Without a Future Queen in Sight." Diana Spencer, whom he wed in 1981, made our cover 87 times, more than any other subject. Now the romance of their son Prince William and Kate Middleton, both 24, is hot copy. Only time will tell whether they will have a happy ending. In the meantime, we offer you a peek into the lives of royals around the world. Enjoy the view.

A CENTURY
of STYLE

Transcending the stodgy looks dictated by tradition and protocol, a handful of royals have reigned over that most difficult of conquests: the world of fashion. From the Duke of Windsor and his knot to the effortless elegance of Monaco's Grace to the immortal glamour of Diana, these aristocrats of chic have kept royalty the object of fascination long after they have faded into history

THE POWER OF LOOKING GOOD
Diana's "Elvis Dress," a stunning beaded sheath by Catherine Walker. Worn during an '89 Hong Kong official visit, the actual inspiration wasn't the King of Rock 'n' Roll but Queen Elizabeth I.

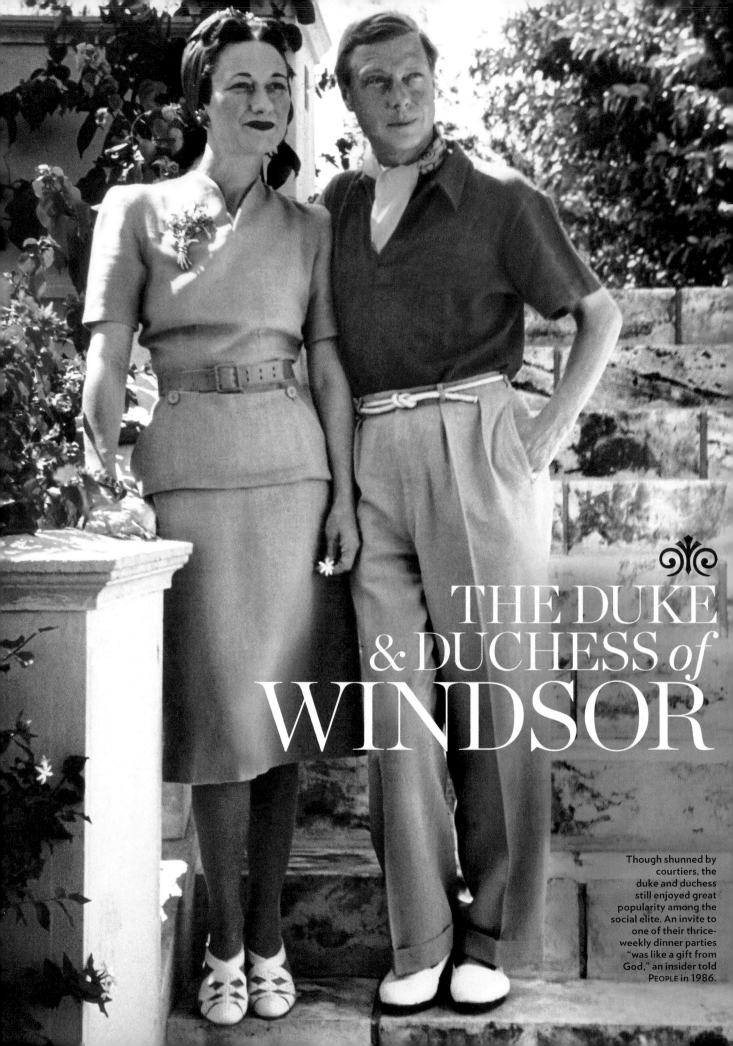

THE DUKE
& DUCHESS *of*
WINDSOR

Though shunned by courtiers, the duke and duchess still enjoyed great popularity among the social elite. An invite to one of their thrice-weekly dinner parties "was like a gift from God," an insider told PEOPLE in 1986.

THE WINDSOR KNOT
The duke's most famous fashion legacy was his namesake tie knot (left). But the ex-King didn't care for the style, preferring the narrower four-in-hand knot for his neckwear.

They were a scandalous couple whose love affair cost him the British crown. But when it came to fashion, at least, Edward VIII and Wallis Simpson—the American divorcée he refused to give up—never put a foot wrong. Named Duke and Duchess of Windsor after he abdicated and they wed in 1937, the pair spent most of the next four decades as royal outcasts in a mansion in Neuilly, outside Paris. But these exiles lived in sublime style. The Baltimore-bred duchess, who famously said, "A woman can't be too rich or too thin," accentuated her narrow frame with sharply tailored suits from Mainbocher, Dior, Chanel and Givenchy. Among her trademarks: high-necked evening gowns, knee-length skirts and dazzling gems. Little wonder she made international Best Dressed lists for more than 40 years. For his part, Edward, a consummate English dandy, cut a dapper figure in made-to-measure suits and popularized a foppish look for golf: baggy plusfours and a riot of plaids, checks and stripes. Their 35-year union was marked by extravagant parties and a seemingly limitless clothing budget. "It was a fairytale life," Jean-Pierre Auge, the couple's former chef, told PEOPLE. "But they lived it very well."

"I'm nothing to look at, so the only thing I can do is dress better than anyone else"

—THE DUCHESS OF WINDSOR

The Jewels of a Duchess

Wallis Simpson would never become queen, but she accessorized herself like one. Her jewelry collection is still considered legendary. After her death, Sotheby's auctioned off many of the prized gems for charity, including the insignia Prince of Wales brooch the duke had made for her around 1935. Rumor has it that a bidding war ensued between Prince Charles, intent on giving it to his wife, Diana, and Elizabeth Taylor, who called into the auction while poolside at her L.A. home. A longtime friend of the Windsors', Taylor had admired the plume of pavé-set diamond feathers for decades and won the pin with a $623,000 bid. "I knew the duchess wanted me to have it," she wrote in her book *My Love Affair with Jewelry*. "It's a royal piece that I save for very special occasions."

Always well turned out, the couple even adorned their four pugs with mink collars and gold Cartier leashes and spritzed them with Christian Dior perfume. "They had nothing else really to do except worry about how they looked," fashion writer Kathleen Craughwell-Varda later told PEOPLE.

FIT *for a* QUEEN

*The Queen Mother's famed White Wardrobe caused a sensation
and proved to be her fashion legacy*

"It was an iconic moment in royal style. She was like an actress. And she assumed the role"

The Queen's fairy-tale dresses inspired the Paris designers and brightened bleak times.

In later life few would have mistaken the Windsors' beloved Queen Mum—who died in 2002 at age 101—for a trendsetter. But the mother of Britain's Queen Elizabeth II was a master of power dressing. As queen consort to King George VI, the former Lady Elizabeth Bowes-Lyon helped lift the nation's spirits when she asked Norman Hartnell in 1938 to create what would ultimately be known as the White Wardrobe, a series of alabaster ensembles for a state visit to France. Shortly before the trip Elizabeth's mother died, and Hartnell scrambled to find an alternative for mourning black. He decided on ivory dresses inspired by royal portraits. The romantic dresses caused a sensation in France, and Hartnell's innovations made him a star among royal dressmakers. His patron's Victorian-influenced gowns of crinoline, lace and embroidery cemented her unique style; whether it was soft pastels or feather-plume hats, the Queen Mum stayed faithful to her signature look. "It was an iconic moment in royal style," says royals biographer Hugo Vickers, the author of *Elizabeth, the Queen Mother.* "She was like an actress. And she assumed the role."

The Queen Mum (at 80 in 1980) stayed true to her whimsical look.

Elizabeth commissioned society photographer Cecil Beaton to document her White Wardrobe on the grounds of Buckingham Palace in 1939.

the JET-SET PRINCESS

Long before Prince Harry made tabloid headlines, his great-aunt Margaret (1930-2002) was the wild Windsor. With a tortoiseshell cigarette holder in one hand and a tumbler of Famous Grouse whiskey in the other, Queen Elizabeth's kid sister became an It Girl for dreary 1950s Britain and conquered London nightlife with pals who included Elizabeth Taylor, Peter Sellers and Noël Coward. A fan of Dior's, Margaret disdained the buttoned-down look favored by the Queen and other royals, and by the swinging '60s was turning heads in miniskirts and psychedelic prints. But a flair for fashion couldn't mask a life plagued by unhappiness and confusion about her royal role. Still, Princess Margaret remains a style icon today, inspiring the spring/summer 2006 Burberry Prorsum collection with rich brocade coats, elegant silk shirts and sophisticated dresses.

PRINCESS
MARGARET

While her sister, the Queen, loved horses and hunting, Margaret (in '56) preferred clothes shopping and nights on the town. "My aunt was . . . incredibly vital and attractive when she was young," recalled Prince Charles.

The flamboyant princess (in '69, during one of her frequent visits to the island of Mustique) loved wild prints like this vibrant caftan.

"She had such a wonderfully free spirit. She loved life and lived it to the full," her nephew Prince Charles said.

Flouting royal etiquette by embracing a glamorous lifestyle, Margaret (in '67) once said, "Disobedience is my joy."

"I can't imagine anything more wonderful than being who I am"

—PRINCESS MARGARET

nscreen and off, she was grace itself. Born to a rich Philadelphia family, Grace Patricia Kelly gained fame as an actress and the embodiment of American style: pearls, white gloves, cashmere twinsets, cinched waists and long full skirts that fashion editors quickly dubbed the Grace Kelly look. A devotee of Christian Dior, Oleg Cassini and Hollywood costume designers Edith Head and Helen Rose (who would later create her wedding dress), she exuded a cool sophistication that became the essence of '50s chic. But after a meteoric Hollywood rise (fresh from New York, the former model made her first picture in 1951, at 22, and four years later collected a Best Actress Oscar for *The Country Girl*), she tired of films. "I don't want to dress up a picture with just my face," Kelly once said of a career that often called for her to play little more than a decorative high-society blonde. Instead, she went on to conquer the heart of Prince Rainier III of Monaco, ruler of a tiny principality and among the world's most eligible bachelors. After a whirlwind courtship, the pair starred in a lavish April 1956 wedding not unlike a Hollywood blockbuster. The movie star bride put Monaco on the map, and though she always conveyed a natural nobility, she soon mastered a new role: Her Serene Highness. As Princess Grace, she fused new-world ease to old-world haute couture, adding lavish ball gowns, crisp suits and even turbans to her wardrobe. To her fans' dismay, Grace never returned to acting—but she never left the headlines. At 51, the princess was turning heads in a straw hat and purple gown at the 1981 wedding of Prince Charles and Diana Spencer. A year later she was dead—the victim of a car accident near the same twisting Riviera corniches she and Cary Grant drove in Hitchcock's *To Catch a Thief*. By then she'd earned fashion immortality and, in 1990, was chosen one of the most stylish people in history by the International Best Dressed Poll. The secret to her unsurpassed elegance, according to Cassini, a former beau: "She dressed like a lady."

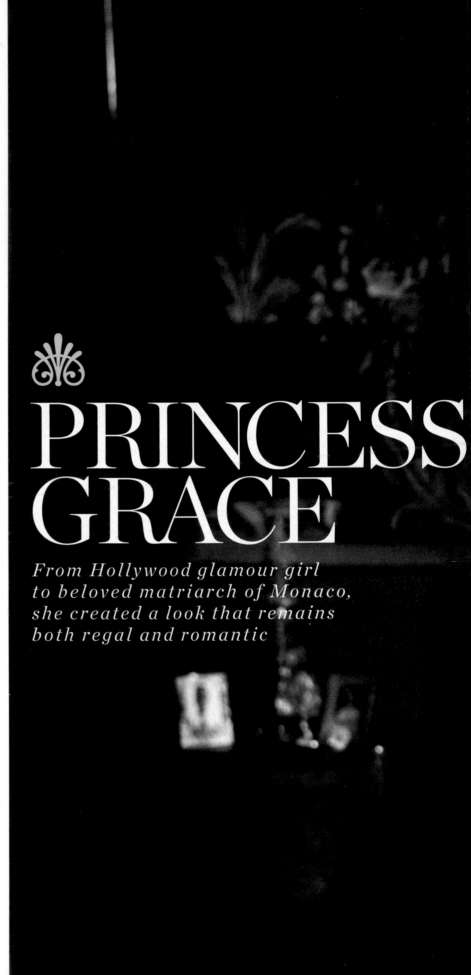

PRINCESS GRACE

From Hollywood glamour girl to beloved matriarch of Monaco, she created a look that remains both regal and romantic

Grace (in 1969) always projected aristocratic elegance. After her marriage to Rainier, she turned her back on Hollywood and devoted herself to promoting her adopted homeland, Monaco.

"She wanted to be
remembered as a lady.
And that's precisely
what she was"
—PHOTOGRAPHER HOWELL CONANT

THE PRINCESS
AND THE BAG

So adored was Princess Grace that when she used her oversize crocodile-skin Hermès bag to demurely conceal her pregnancy during a 1956 U.S. visit, the accessory became an immediate must-have. The company was so grateful to the princess, who also toted the boxy purse during a LIFE magazine cover shoot, they called it the Kelly bag. It remains a perennial bestseller: Hermès maintains a one-year waiting list for the item. According to legend, even Princess Diana had to wait six months for a powder-blue ostrich-skin version of the coveted Hermès classic.

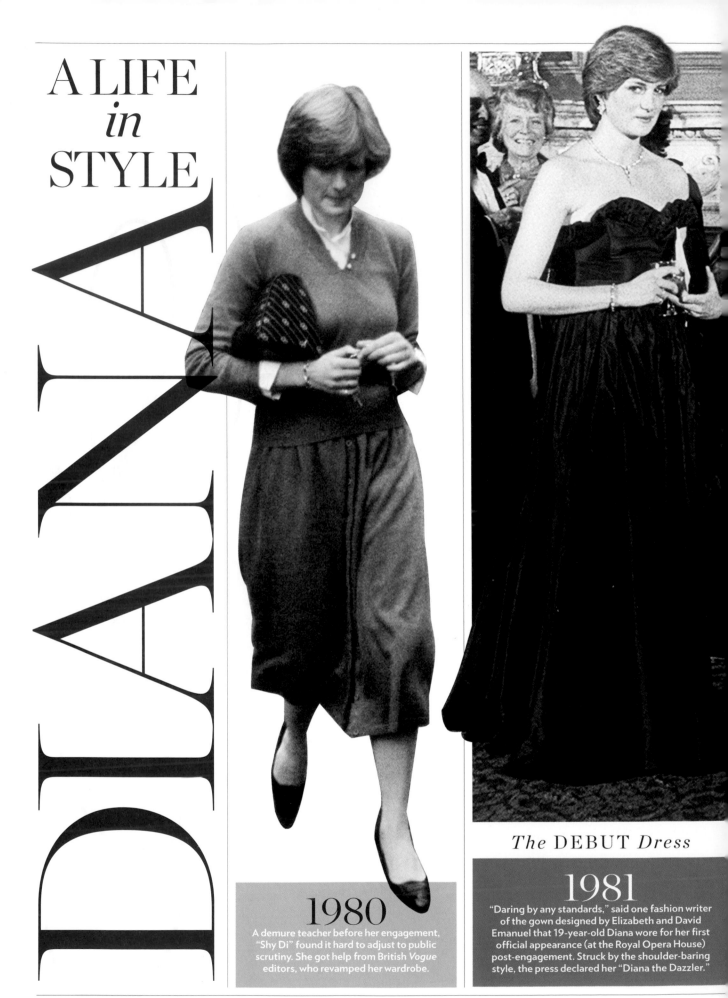

A LIFE *in* STYLE

DIANA

The DEBUT *Dress*

1980

A demure teacher before her engagement, "Shy Di" found it hard to adjust to public scrutiny. She got help from British *Vogue* editors, who revamped her wardrobe.

1981

"Daring by any standards," said one fashion writer of the gown designed by Elizabeth and David Emanuel that 19-year-old Diana wore for her first official appearance (at the Royal Opera House) post-engagement. Struck by the shoulder-baring style, the press declared her "Diana the Dazzler."

1982

Less than three months after giving birth to William, Diana tipped her hat to tradition with this Scottish look at the Braemar Games near Balmoral.

1983

After Diana was photographed wearing the lamb line-up sweater at a polo club in June 1983, a knitwear company sold $1 million worth of the design.

1984

During her second pregnancy, Diana turned to designer Jan Vanvelden for comfortable maternity wear. This outfit was remade for her after she gave birth.

1985

When Charles and Diana visited Australia, the princess turned heads in Nancy Reagan red.

1986

Diana looked regal as she presented the new Colours to the Royal Hampshire Regiment's 1st Battalion.

1987

Diana (in her oft-worn spectator pumps) bared the royal knees in a pouf skirt by the Emanuels.

1988

Diana blossomed in a floral silk taffeta Catherine Walker gown at the *Crocodile Dundee II* premiere in London.

The ELVIS *Dress*

1989

This pearl-and-sequin-studded silk gown with a bolero jacket worn in Hong Kong brought to mind Elvis Presley's Las Vegas outfits. Designer Catherine Walker said she "chose pearls because they seemed so appropriate for a visit to the Orient."

1990

For an exhibition of Italian art and furniture in London, Diana put a tartan twist on a '90s must: a long tailored jacket over a knee-length skirt.

1991

For a visit to Royal Air Force bases in Lincolnshire and South Yorkshire, Diana sported what became a wardrobe staple: elegant suiting in bold designs.

1992

A boldly striped Catherine Walker hat and bouclé wool jacket paired with a navy-blue velvet skirt showcased Diana's style at a wedding in Hertfordshire.

1993

Diana upstaged a performance of *The Magic Flute* at a London charity gala in a silk Catherine Walker dress with a bodice adorned with pearl and glass bead flowers.

The REVENGE *Dress*

1994

Capturing attention in a sexy fishtail dress at a *Vanity Fair* gala, Diana stole Charles's thunder the night he admitted infidelity on TV. "I can't think of anyone," said writer Dominick Dunne, "who has [her] ability to stun a crowd by simply entering a room."

1995

The leggy princess brightened Liverpool Women's Hospital in a tangerine-colored Catherine Walker suit. "I am absolutely gobsmacked," said one awed onlooker.

1996

The vibrant Grecian-style Versace gown Diana wore at a benefit in Sydney wowed Sting, who serenaded the princess with "Every Breath You Take."

1997

Strolling into a performance of *Swan Lake* at the English National Ballet, Diana sparkled in a Jacques Azagury minidress studded with bugle beads.

When Caroline Louise Marguerite Grimaldi was born Jan. 23, 1957, Princess Grace's father remarked, "Oh shucks, I wanted a boy." Perhaps as payback for that remark, his eldest grandchild grew up to epitomize ultra-feminine glamour. By the time she was 18, Caroline of Monaco was a regular in the rarefied salons of such Paris couturiers as Dior, Chloé, Valentino and Ungaro. But it was designer Karl Lagerfeld of Chanel who took the princess for his muse, dressing her in ladylike suits by day and glamorous gowns at night. "[Karl] is my favorite," she said. Since 1984 Caroline has worn her friend's creations frequently; the partnership even garnered her a spot in the Fashion Hall of Fame. "It's very important for a princess to make people dream," said a French magazine writer in 1993. "Caroline gives them something to dream about."

GROWING UP GRACEFULLY Like Grace, the princess (in 1980, at 23) has a face the camera loves, with vivid blue eyes, long brown hair and olive complexion. Her father, Prince Rainier III, once said of her stunning looks, "She's very beautiful, just lovely."

SWEET CAROLINE

The elder daughter of Monaco's Prince and his glamorous movie-star bride grew into a breathtaking Continental beauty

In 1965 an 8-year-old Caroline was all smiles for her official royal portrait at the Monaco Palace.

During a 2004 visit to Spain, Caroline made a dramatic entrance in a black-and-white Chanel gown designed by Karl Lagerfeld, her longtime fashion guru and friend.

At the Grimaldi's biggest charity event, the annual Red Cross Ball, 17-year-old Caroline was already a vision in 1974.

"Her elegance is something she was born with"

—KARL LAGERFELD

WHO DRESSES THE QUEEN?

She's the Queen of England, and also, perhaps, of fashion paradox: Who else, in the history of couture, has so perfectly combined pizzazz and tradition? There's method in her mode: In a crowd the Queen wants to be easily seen, but not to be seen as aloof or lording it over her subjects. Her signature accessory? Hats. British betting parlors take wagers on what color topper the Queen will wear to Ladies Day at Ascot. But she is never less than regal. Said designer Miuccia Prada: The Queen "is, simply, one of the most elegant women in the world."

THE MILLINER

For berets, bonnets, turbans and toques, she turns to Philip Somerville. The rules for making her majesty's chapeau: It must stand out, cannot hide her face and, most importantly, "has to stay on in any calamity," said Somerville.

THE GLOVEMISTRESS

Though not formally appointed until the '80s, Cornelia James first crafted a pair of "going away" gloves for then-Princess Elizabeth to wear after her 1947 wedding. When she died in '99, her daughter Genevieve (above) took over.

THE PURSE PURVEYOR

The London-based Launer has supplied the Queen's handbags for the past 40 years. The ubiquitous bags reportedly are used to send coded messages to staff. According to palace lore, if a purse dangles loosely from her left arm, all is well. But if the Queen switches her handbag to the right, it means she's bored with the person talking to her and needs a rescue.

THE COBBLER

Anello & Davide, the firm that created Dorothy's red slippers for *The Wizard of Oz*, became Elizabeth's shoemaker in 2001 on recommendation of the late Queen Mother, who wore their creations for years.

THE DRESSMAKER

The Queen's official couturier for almost 50 years, Sir Hardy Amies, who died in 2003, crafted hundreds of pastel and candy-colored dresses for her. Though he was proud of the restrained styles he created, "I sometimes wish she had been a bit more of a clothes person," Amies once recalled. As to why Elizabeth never embraced high fashion, he said, "The Queen's attitude is that she must always dress for the occasion, usually for a large mob of middle-class people, towards whom she wishes to seem friendly. There's always something cold and cruel about chic clothes she wants to avoid." These days designers such as Karl-Ludwig Rehse carry on the tradition.

HARDY AMIES

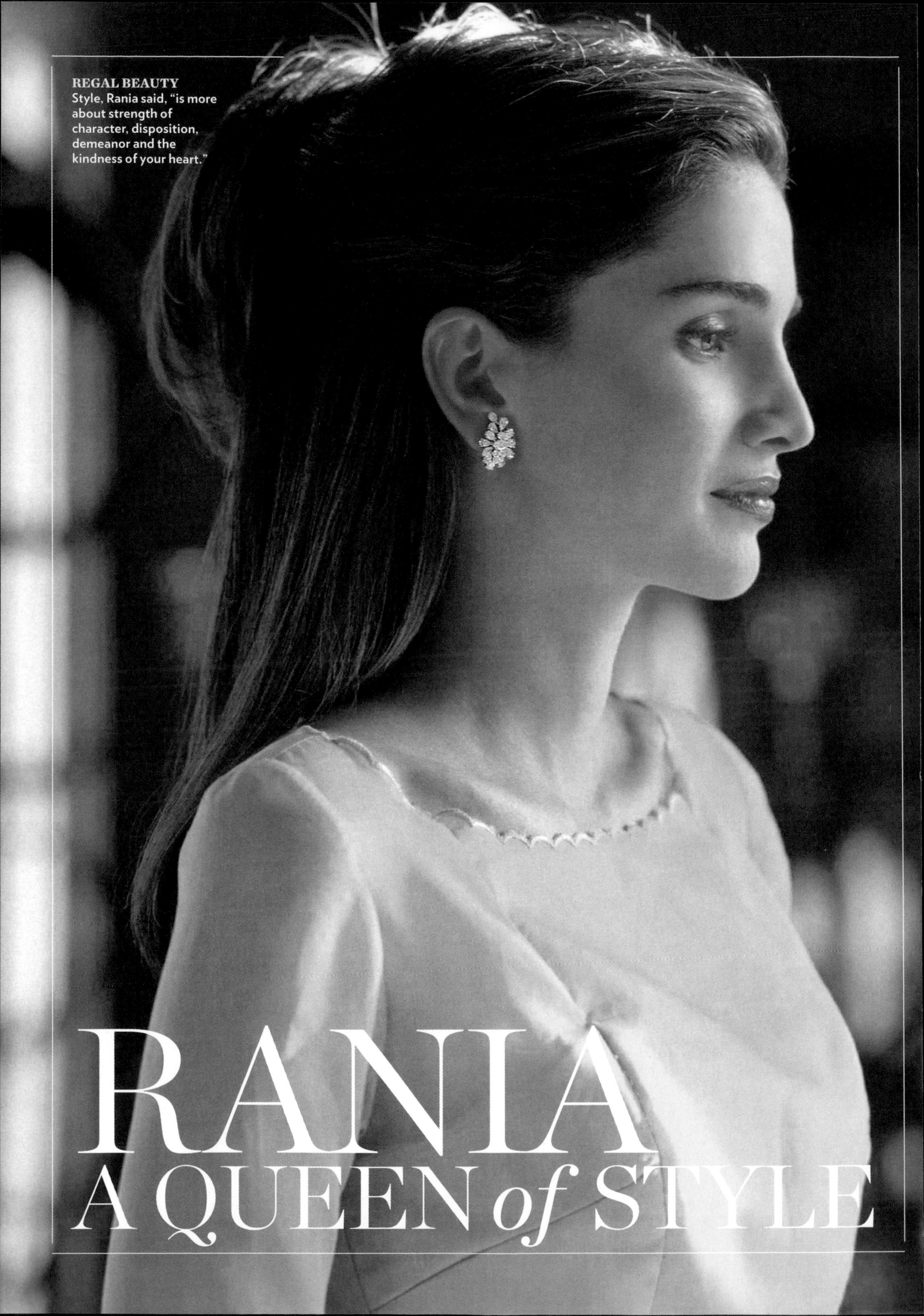

REGAL BEAUTY
Style, Rania said, "is more
about strength of
character, disposition,
demeanor and the
kindness of your heart."

RANIA
A QUEEN *of* STYLE

Thoroughly modern and yet proudly Muslim and Palestinian, Rania of Jordan has helped redefine how the world sees the women of the Middle East. Westerners may debate the role of the veil, but for Rania, 36, the answer is simple: Women should be judged "according to what is going on in their heads, rather than what is on top of their heads." The queen's own look is both daring and respectful of Jordanian values: an alluring array of elegant suits and dramatic gowns from favored designers like Givenchy and Roland Mouret. The wife of King Abdullah and mother of four, says Giorgio Armani, "has the body of a model and holds herself like the queen she is. What more could you want?"

A COMPASSIONATE QUEEN
Rania (visiting a Jordanian village in a safari top and trousers in '06) has used glamour to call attention to the Middle East.

REDEFINING TRADITION

Rania's flair for dressing has been compared to that of Jacqueline Kennedy Onassis and Princess Diana, but the former Apple marketing executive also juggles several demanding roles: hands-on mother, advocate for the developing world and role model for Arab women. "The young relate to her," Maha Khatib of the Jordan River Foundation said of Rania (below, at public appearances in '03, '04 and '05). "She has this ability to maintain her Arabic style with a modern approach."

WHO DRESSES THE PRINCE?

mpeccable tailoring has helped make Prince Charles the king of London's menswear mecca, Savile Row, where high-end shops sometimes bear his royal warrant (a tri-feathered heraldic badge of approval). His look is timeless: sharply cut double-breasted suits, shirts with spread collars, bold rep ties and pocket squares. The prince has single-handedly kept the double-breasted look in fashion since the '80s, but he's not afraid to take a risk, pressing on with linen suits after the press bashed his rumpled appearance. "He couldn't care less," says his former personal tailor Thomas Mahon. "He even ordered another." And the dapper royal's fans aren't just at the palace. In '04 American hip-hop star André 3000 declared, "Prince Charles is my No. 1 British style icon."

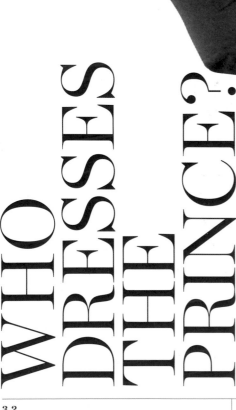

THE ROYAL SHIRTMAKER

Since 1980 Turnbull & Asser has supplied Charles with hand-made cotton shirts and is widely known to now be making his suits—an unexpected choice since the store is owned by Ali Al Fayed, uncle of Diana's late boyfriend Dodi. The shop's customer service may have won the prince over: After one of his polo injuries, they made him one-armed shirts, with matching slings.

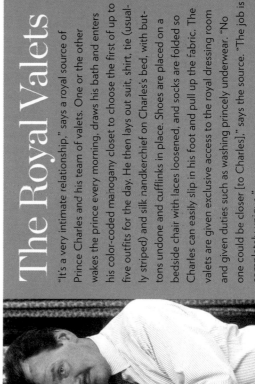

As Colonel of the Welsh Guards, Prince Charles wears this regalia and bearskin hat on ceremonial occasions.

THE ROYAL SUITMAKERS

After two decades of shopping at 133-year-old Anderson & Sheppard, Charles caused a stir when he pulled his warrant in 2003. No reason was given ("The prince's shopping is a matter of personal taste," said a palace spokesman). But former A&S tailor Mahon suspects Charles's lack of time for the two or three fittings required for their $5,000 bespoke creations led to dissatisfaction: "You only get one fitting with Prince Charles." Charles now wears Turnbull & Asser ready-made suits constructed from a template. "You can tell by the lapels," sniffs Mahon. "A good handmade suit has an understated class."

THE ROYAL COBBLER

Taking a cue from his parents, Prince Charles awarded a royal warrant to the shoe store John Lobb, which measures and outlines customers' feet before making a wooden replica to design perfectly fitting footwear. Style icon Jacqueline Kennedy Onassis bought Lobb's traditional riding boots, some of whose styles are 140 years old. Men's leather shoes start at $3,800. Order them in the spring and they'll be ready by fall.

The Royal Valets

"It's a very intimate relationship," says a royal source of Prince Charles and his team of valets. One or the other wakes the prince every morning, draws his bath and enters his color-coded mahogany closet to choose the first of up to five outfits for the day. He then lays out suit, shirt, tie (usually striped) and silk handkerchief on Charles's bed, with buttons undone and cufflinks in place. Shoes are placed on a bedside chair with laces loosened, and socks are folded so Charles can easily slip in his foot and pull up the fabric. The valets are given exclusive access to the royal dressing room and given duties such as washing princely underwear. "No one could be closer [to Charles]," says the source. "The job is completely unique."

Former valet Ken Stronach (in '86) arranges medals on Charles's naval wear in the Uniform Room at Kensington Palace.

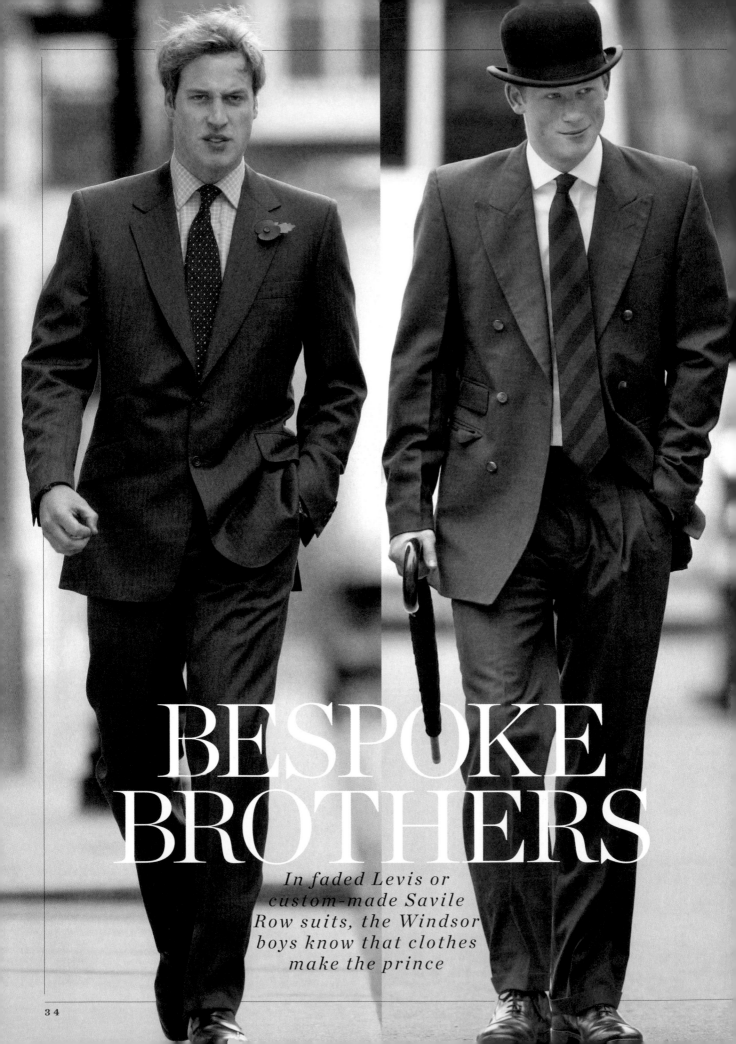

BESPOKE
BROTHERS

In faded Levis or custom-made Savile Row suits, the Windsor boys know that clothes make the prince

Princes Harry and William, fashion plates? On most days the dressed-down brothers would hardly look out of place on an Ivy League campus. Despite royal titles and the privileges that come with them, the princes live in a knockabout wardrobe of denim, rugby shirts, fleece vests and broken-in riding boots (albeit very expensive ones). But when sartorial duty calls, the princes know a good tailor. At Prince Charles's 2005 wedding to Camilla, the young men stole the spotlight from the newlyweds in bespoke morning suits by Gieves & Hawkes paired with family-heirloom tie pins, and they are equally at ease in made-to-measure blazers as their ubiquitous polo jerseys. At 15, William ranked No. 1 on the annual International Best-Dressed Poll, which lauded him for inspiring "a fresh, younger classicism among Savile Row tailors," and Harry was named a Best-Dressed Brit in 2001 after pairing a lavender pin-striped tie with a dark suit for Prince Philip's 80th-birthday party. The flair for natty attire must be in the DNA; the boys have followed in Charles's well-shod footsteps to Turnbull & Asser, where they buy custom-made shirts and silk ties. But their individual takes on fashion mirror their personalities: William, 24, favors preppy looks from Ralph Lauren and Burberry, supplier of his cherished wool crew-neck pullovers. (Not that Will is all tradition: His penchant for silver wraparound sunglasses sparked a run on the style in the late '90s.) Harry, 21, is more kicked back, favoring weathered logo tees, athletic wear and outdoorsy looks from hip Australian label Zanerobe. The younger prince accents his looks with jewelry given him by Zimbabwean girlfriend Chelsy Davy: His beaded leather bracelet matches one she owns, and a wooden ring hangs from a string around his neck. But no matter what they wear, the princes may have the ultimate advantage when it comes to looking good. "They are such good-looking boys," says *Harper's Bazaar* fashion director Alison Edmond. "They can get away with anything."

Far left: A sophisticated Prince William suited up for a day of work at London's HSBC Bank, where he gained financial know-how during an '05 internship. To his right, Sandhurst graduate Prince Harry walked in a May '05 army veterans parade, like 2,000 other soldiers, wearing a bowler hat.

THE BANGLE BOYS

Once, the only jewelry fit for a princely wrist was a Rolex. But in 1999 Prince William was spotted wearing three bracelets made of gold, copper and elephant hair—souvenirs from a Botswana holiday—on his right wrist. The trinkets have been a wardrobe staple since, joined by a Lance Armstrong LiveStrong bracelet and a band in support of the British & Irish Lions rugby team. His kid brother is also fond of arm candy: After an '04 African jaunt, Harry sported four-inch stacks of copper, brass and colorful thread. William (left) wore a bracelet at St. Andrews University in November '04, while Harry (right) spruced up his wrist at a July '06 polo game.

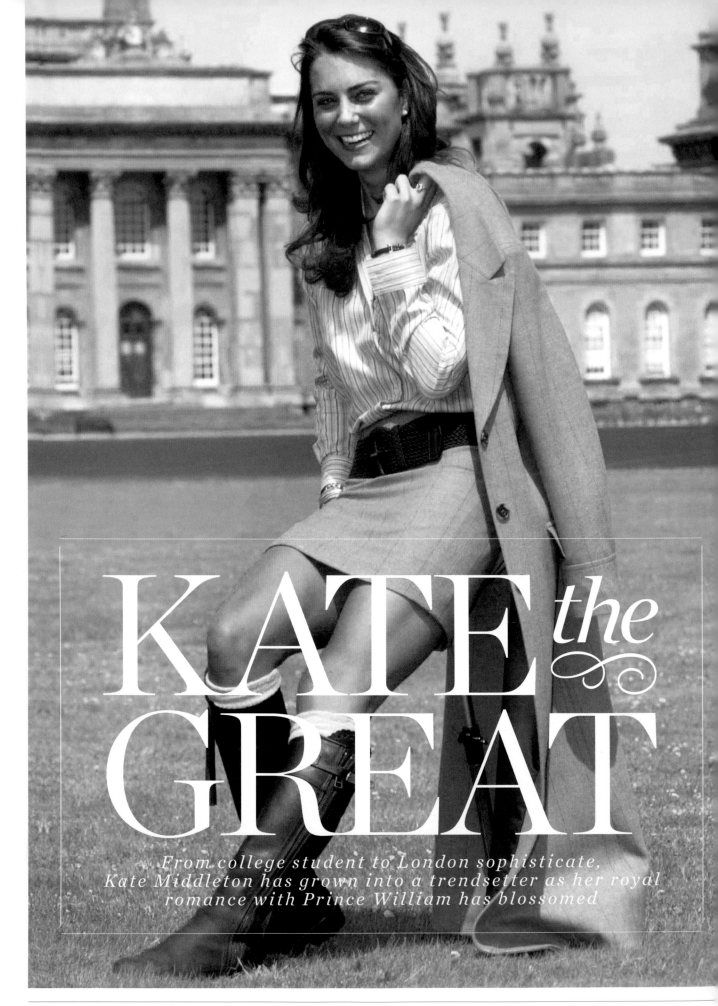

KATE *the* GREAT

From college student to London sophisticate, Kate Middleton has grown into a trendsetter as her royal romance with Prince William has blossomed

A beaming Kate modeled for a British clothing company at Oxfordshire's Blenheim Palace in 2004 (far left). When Laura Parker Bowles wed on May 6, 2006, Kate sported a delicate hat (left) and a tan from a Caribbean holiday with her prince. A year earlier she had made what amounted to a royal debut at the wedding of William's close friend Hugh van Cutsem (below). Braving the paparazzi for the first time, "she looked radiant," said royals writer Judy Wade. "As if she knew something we didn't."

When Kate Middleton first caught the public eye in March 2002, her outfit caused a stir. Walking the runway for a charity fashion show at Scotland's University of St. Andrews, the amateur model wore a sheer black sheath over a bandeau top and bikini bottom. Seated in the front row? A captivated Prince William, whom she had met when they entered college the same year.

Since then, Kate's relationship with the prince has grown from friendship (the pair, both now 24, moved off-campus with two pals sophomore year) to tender romance, confirmed in April '04, when they were photographed cozying up on a Swiss ski trip. And as the English rose's role in the prince's life changed, so did her style. In her teens, high school friend Gemma Williamson says, Kate—whose parents own a mail-order party-goods store—"looked good by wearing standard stuff." By university, she was casual but posh in Miss Sixty

THE NEW ROYAL TRENDSETTERS

Once, a well-born young lady was confined to crinoline and taffeta. Not anymore. Harry's girlfriend Chelsy Davy (left, at an '06 polo match) loves minis and tank tops; Princess Anne's rebellious daughter Zara Phillips (middle) shocked her elders with her pierced tongue. And Kate (right) updates her classic looks with halter tops and plunging necklines.

Kate and William flirted at a June '05 polo match in Gloucestershire, where the prince bought his gal an ice-cream cone.

"She is a natural"

—A PALACE INSIDER

jeans. After she entered royal circles, Kate adopted a sophisticated look with Longchamp bags, miniskirts that showed off legs toned by years of field hockey and tennis, and locks highlighted at Richard Ward's London salon with "chocolate chunks and caramel slices," says an acquaintance. At heart, Kate remained an unfussy product of England's Home Counties, her ever-present knee-high riding boots symbolizing her love of horses, hounds and shooting parties—a plus for William, an avid hunter who has said, "I am a country boy at heart."

Mixing edgy trends with a classic British look, Kate radiates the air of a modern princess. At the June 4, 2005 wedding of William's longtime pal, management consultant Hugh van Cutsem, she wore a conservative white jacket and knee-length skirt. But her Philip Treacy hat gave "a funky edge to an otherwise simple ensemble," noted celebrity stylist Jill Wanless. She impressed observers by composing herself to smile in the face of the paparazzi—a test, declares royals writer Judy Wade, that "she passed."

The following March Kate seemed to clear another bar: She was invited to sit with Charles and Camilla in their box at the Cheltenham horse races and turned heads in a beige herringbone and brown velvet Katherine Hooker jacket, topped with a brown fur hat that evoked Julie Christie's Lara in *Dr. Zhivago.* Two months later her position in the inner circle was sealed: At the wedding of William's stepsister Laura Parker Bowles, Kate wore a chic cream-and-gold embroidered coat. An onlooker noted, "She is a natural."

Now the world waits to see if Kate's wardrobe will include a tiara or two. A friend cautions, "They're young," but Wade says, "They had a couple of idyllic years in St. Andrews. I expect he won't wait too long [to propose]." Until then, pal Williamson points out, Kate sparkles on her own: "William really has picked an absolute diamond."

A MODERN GIRL ENTERS THE ROYAL WORLD

Now living part-time in London and launching a kids' clothing line, Kate teamed a bright scarf with a street-smart skirt for a Feb. 9, 2006, day of shopping along the King's Road (left). At a June 3, 2006, charity event for pediatric medical research (center), she was a knockout in a BCBG jersey gown. For a horse show at Princess Anne's estate Gatcombe Park on Aug. 6, 2005 (right), she jazzed up Seven for All Mankind jeans and her trademark Spanish leather Really Wild Clothing Company boots with a vintage cowboy hat from Manhattan's Screaming Mimi's.

"Royals love hats," says Irish milliner Philip Treacy, now the exclusive hat designer for Camilla, Duchess of Cornwall. "They add a sprinkle of style, elegance, beauty and panache. They just make people smile."

TOPPING IT OFF

For royal weddings, birthdays or a day at the races, a well-born lady just isn't dressed without a proper hat

TRUE BLUE
A crown of feathers was among several eye-popping hats Treacy designed for Camilla in 2005.

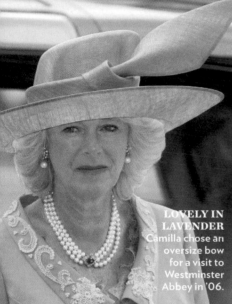

LOVELY IN LAVENDER
Camilla chose an oversize bow for a visit to Westminster Abbey in '06.

LUCK OF THE ENGLISH
The duchess celebrated St. Patrick's Day in high style.

HEAD CASES

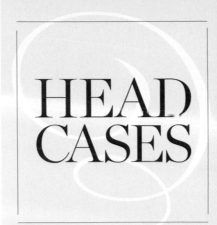

1. Princess Anne's daughter Zara. Phillips wore a fedora-inspired number to Ladies' Day at Royal Ascot in 2002.
2. Princess Beatrice wore a vivid blue topper to church in 2003.
3. Sophie, Countess of Wessex, wore an Easter top hat in 2000.
4. For the wedding of her mother and Prince Charles, Laura Parker Bowles wore a gilded design.
5. Princess Maxima of the Netherlands chose a broad-brimmed hat for a 2004 royal wedding in Spain.
6. Sweden's Princess Victoria wore cardinal red to a papal Mass in 2005.

JEWELS

Shimmering tiaras, medieval crowns, dazzling gems hundreds of years old: The priceless treasures of the world's monarchies are as fabled as the dynasties that have possessed them. This unique store, passed down through generations, reveals an extraordinary history told by a sparkling array of precious stones

NICE HAT!
Britain's Imperial State Crown is carried from the House of Lords after Her Majesty's annual address to Parliament.

All the
QUEEN'S
CROWNS

*What becomes Her Majesty most? The gleaming
collection of royal diadems that have adorned the
head of Elizabeth II since childhood*

The George IV Diadem

Pictured on British postage stamps, the delicate crown is a piece of royal treasure commoners can literally get their hands on. More than 169 pearls and 1,333 diamonds in the shape of crosses and the national floral emblems of roses, thistles and shamrocks make it a national treasure. Dating back to 1820, a time when critics deemed it too effeminate for George IV, the crown was first worn by Queen Victoria, who attended almost every formal occasion in the diamond headpiece. The present Queen (left, in 1952) is not quite so attached to the bauble, though she does wear the diadem to the House of Lords for the opening of Parliament each November. That annual appearance—plus the daily mail—ensure more people see the George IV diadem than any other item of royal jewelry.

3,174 Gems
The crown sparkles with 2,868 diamonds, 273 pearls, 17 sapphires, 11 emeralds and 5 rubies.

The Imperial State Crown

In a collection of jewels full of superlatives, Britain's Imperial State Crown may outdo them all. The gold frame holds some 3,000 gems set in silver. Front and center lies the 317.4-carat Cullinan II diamond, second in size only to the Cullinan I diamond, another stunner, found in the Royal Scepter. Named for the African mine in which they were discovered in 1905, the 11 major Cullinan stones and hundreds of fragments were cut from the largest gem-quality diamond ever found. Just above the spectacular Cullinan II sits the Black Prince's Ruby, which has belonged to the monarchy since it was given to its namesake Edward of Woodstock in 1367. But the most storied of all the stones, the St. Edward's Sapphire, takes its place atop the cross. Historians believe the shimmering gem once adorned the 1043 coronation ring of Edward the Confessor. In spite of their splendor, these awe-inspiring jewels appear just once a year, when Her Majesty opens Parliament (left).

The Mother & Daughter Crowns

An 11-year-old Princess Elizabeth would have to wait more than a decade to officially take her place on the throne, but the gilded trappings of the monarchy came her way as soon as her father, King George VI, and his wife, Queen Elizabeth, were crowned. Just like her parents, little Lilibet received a gleaming headpiece of her own for their May 1937 coronation. At the moment her mother was made Queen, she and her younger sister Margaret donned miniature medieval-looking circlets. Though the girls' grandmother Queen Mary would later write in her journal that the two "looked too sweet . . . especially when they put on their coronets," the silk-lined, silver-gilt trinket (below left), fashioned by the royal family's jeweler Garrard & Co., accentuated Elizabeth's already regal air. The youngster greeted the British public from the balcony of Buckingham Palace alongside her mother, who wore a spectacular platinum crown specially made for the ceremony. The Queen Mum would have many occasions to wear her coronet through the years, though none more special than when she again watched her daughter Elizabeth become Queen 16 years later.

The crown of Queen Elizabeth, the Queen Mother, shimmers with precious stones and contains the Koh-i-Noor, once the world's largest cut diamond. Set in the center of the headpiece, the 105.6-carat gem, whose name means Mountain of Light in Persian, was thought to bring bad luck to men who possessed it. Not so for women like the hearty Queen Mum, who died at age 101. The gem shone brightly in the crown atop her casket after her death in 2002 (left).

The St. Edward's Crown

On June 2, 1953, before 8,251 guests and dignitaries from 129 nations seated in Westminster Abbey, the Archbishop of Canterbury uttered words first spoken in 973: "God crown you with a crown of glory and righteousness . . ." With that, he placed a diadem first used in 1661 by Charles II on the head of 27-year-old Elizabeth, formally installing her as head of the British Commonwealth 16 months after the death of her father. Though certainly not the most valuable of Crown Jewels, (which include the George IV Diadem and the Imperial State Crown), the St. Edward's, as the coronation crown, eclipses all others in importance. Named for a famed Anglo-Saxon monarch and dotted with 444 precious stones, the foot-tall, nearly-5-lb. gold behemoth is so unwieldy that Queen Elizabeth practiced wearing it around Buckingham Palace for several weeks before the day of the ceremony. Officially, however, Her Majesty wore the crown for just three hours, the length of her investiture, having exchanged the heavy headpiece for the Imperial Crown to return to Buckingham Palace. The St. Edward's, meanwhile, retook its place in the Tower of London, where it lies in wait until the next sovereign is crowned.

Coronation Classic

Made of gold and ringed by two rows of gold beads, the St. Edward's Crown boasts 16 diamond rosettes, amethysts, pink and green tourmalines, white and yellow topazes and aquamarines.

The 1953 coronation of Queen Elizabeth II in Westminster Abbey.

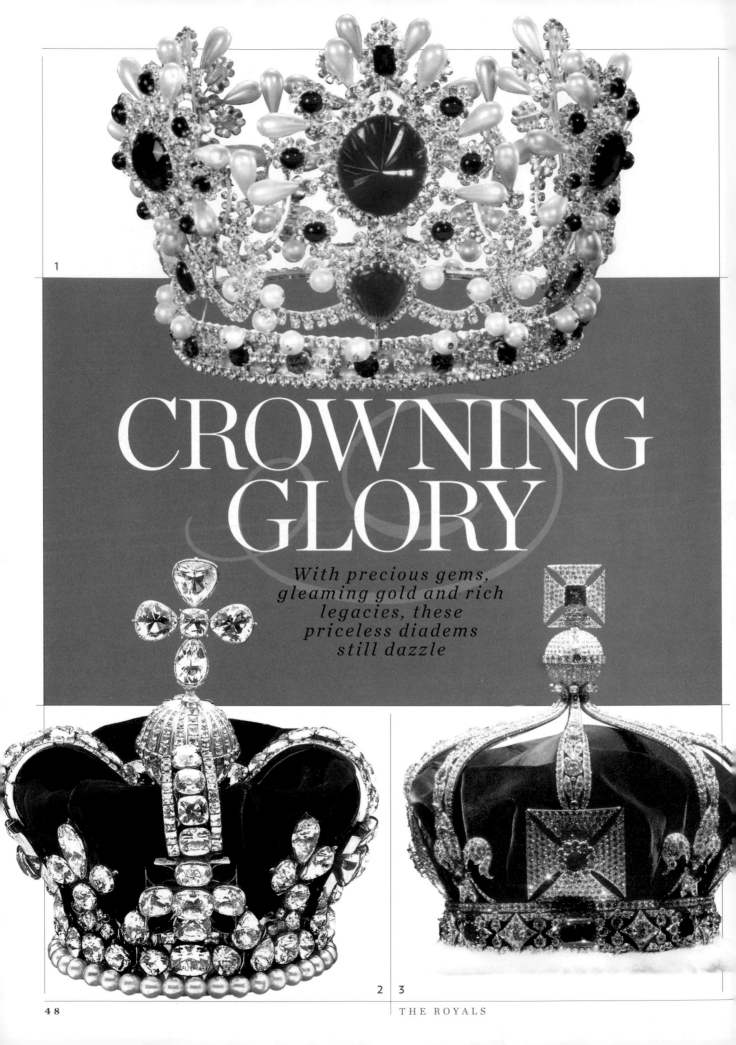

CROWNING GLORY

With precious gems, gleaming gold and rich legacies, these priceless diadems still dazzle

4

5

6

7

8

1. The coronation crown of Iran's Empress Farah Diba, 1967. The Van Cleef & Arpels stunner holds 1,646 stones including emeralds, rubies and pearls. **2.** Crown of Mary of Modena, 1685. Worn by the wife of England's James II, more than 500 diamonds and 129 large pearls dot its gold frame. **3.** Imperial crown of India, 1911. King George V's 2-lb. marvel contains more than 6,100 diamonds. **4.** St. Wenceslas crown, 1347. Part of the Bohemian crown jewels kept in Prague, the 22k gold crown is set with 19 sapphires, 30 emeralds and 20 pearls. **5.** Margaret of York's crown, mid-15th century. This gilded relic is one of two British medieval crowns still in existence. **6.** Crown of the Andes, late 16th century. Legend has it that 24 goldsmiths took six years to make this 22k gold-and-emerald Colombian treasure. **7.** Coronation crown of Queen Adelaide, 1831. The Queen's own gems once filled the frame, which has since held replica stones. **8.** Empress Anna's crown, 18th century. Worn by Russia's ruler from 1730 to 1740 and now kept in the Kremlin.

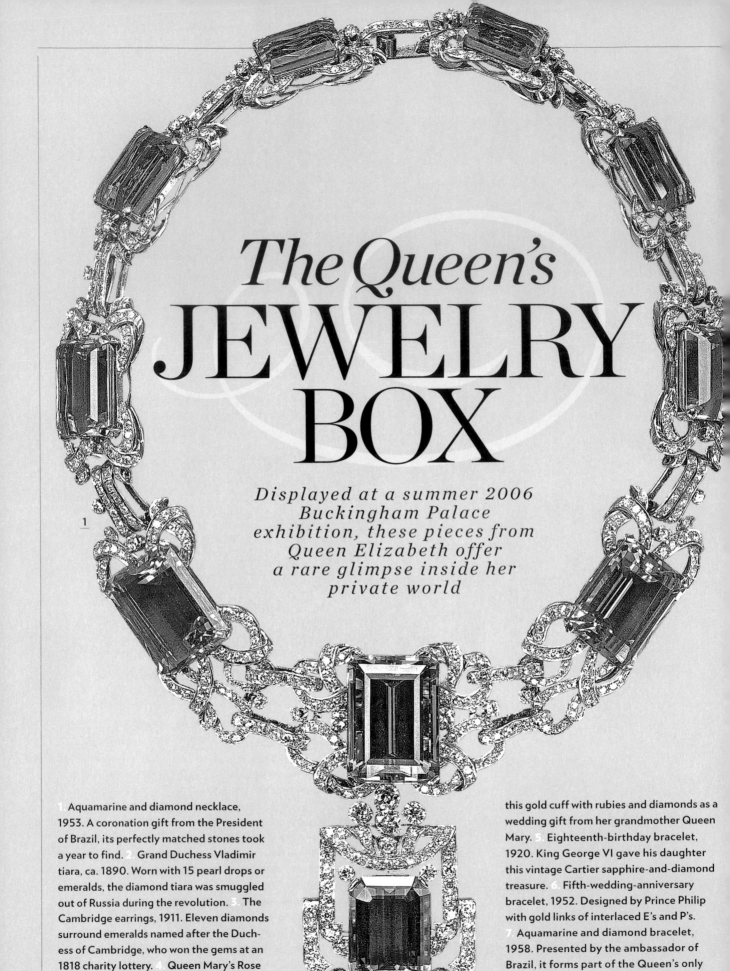

The Queen's JEWELRY BOX

Displayed at a summer 2006 Buckingham Palace exhibition, these pieces from Queen Elizabeth offer a rare glimpse inside her private world

1

1. Aquamarine and diamond necklace, 1953. A coronation gift from the President of Brazil, its perfectly matched stones took a year to find. **2.** Grand Duchess Vladimir tiara, ca. 1890. Worn with 15 pearl drops or emeralds, the diamond tiara was smuggled out of Russia during the revolution. **3.** The Cambridge earrings, 1911. Eleven diamonds surround emeralds named after the Duchess of Cambridge, who won the gems at an 1818 charity lottery. **4.** Queen Mary's Rose of York bracelet, 1893. Elizabeth received

this gold cuff with rubies and diamonds as a wedding gift from her grandmother Queen Mary. **5.** Eighteenth-birthday bracelet, 1920. King George VI gave his daughter this vintage Cartier sapphire-and-diamond treasure. **6.** Fifth-wedding-anniversary bracelet, 1952. Designed by Prince Philip with gold links of interlaced E's and P's. **7.** Aquamarine and diamond bracelet, 1958. Presented by the ambassador of Brazil, it forms part of the Queen's only completely modern set of jewels.

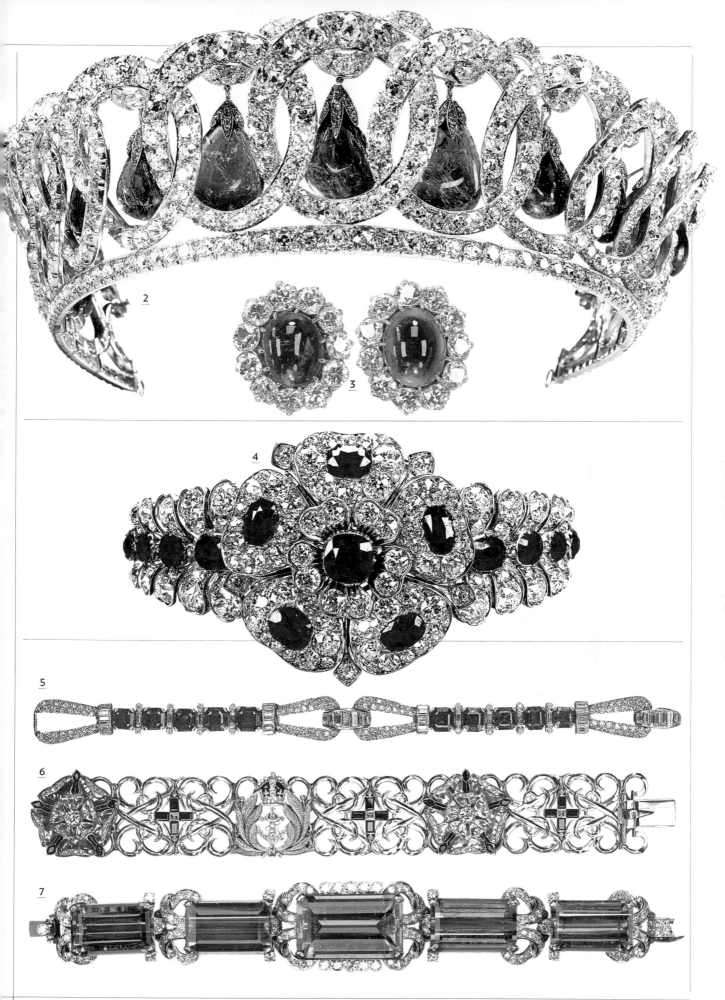

Her Majesty's BRO

Rarely seen without one of her cherished pins, the Queen shows off he

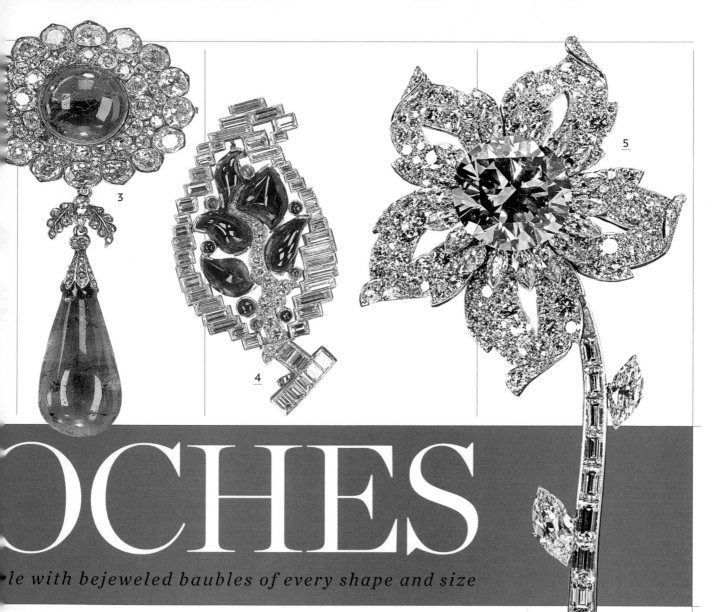

OCHES

le with bejeweled baubles of every shape and size

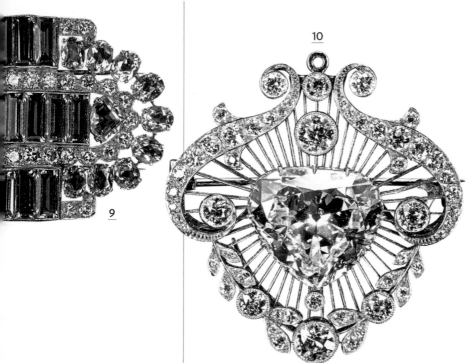

1. True lover's knot, late 19th century. Diamonds set in gold and silver.
2. Flower basket, ca. 1930. Rubies, diamonds, sapphires and emeralds given to mark the 1948 birth of Prince Charles.
3. Emerald-and-diamond pendant, 1911.
4. Queen mother's leaf, ca. 1920. Unique design of sapphires, diamonds, emeralds, amethysts and a ruby.
5. Williamson diamond, 1952. Holds a 23.6-ct. pink diamond. 6. Aquamarine and diamond, 1958. 7. Emerald and diamond, 1911, emerald sparkler with a carved rose. 8. Flower spray, 1945. Cartier pink and blue sapphires.
9. Aquamarine-and-diamond clips, ca. 1940. 10. Cullinan V heart, 1911. The 18.8-ct. middle stone is one of the famed Cullinan diamonds.

A Timeless TREASURE

Forever linked to Princess Diana, the Cambridge Lover's Knot tiara carries the legacy of royal women from ages past

1858
PRINCESS TATIANA
YUSUPOVA OF RUSSIA

c.**1880**
GRAND DUCHESS
AUGUSTA CAROLINE

1957
QUEEN
ELIZABETH II

hen Britain's Queen Mary wanted to design a new tiara in 1914, she found inspiration close to home. Modeling her jewels after diamond tiaras worn by the Romanov Princess Tatiana and Mary's aunt the Grand Duchess Augusta, Mary had 19 diamond arches with drop pearls set on a diamond band. Her creation, called the lover's knot—made with gems she'd received as wedding gifts—was a standout in her priceless collection, now owned by her granddaughter Queen Elizabeth II. But only when it rested on the head of Princess Diana, who received the diadem in 1981 as a wedding present, was the tiara's power to enchant truly felt

1983
PRINCESS DIANA

The day before Diana married Prince Charles, her future mother-in-law handed her a red leather box. Inside lay the storied Lover's Knot tiara, once worn by the Queen's grandmother Mary and passed down through three royal generations. But that morning Diana's mind wasn't on the jewelry's legacy. Using a nickname given to the Queen by the British press, she was said to have shouted with glee, "I have Brenda's rocks!"

WEDDINGS

ENGLAND, 1981 Prince Charles and Diana Spencer took their trip to the altar at St. Paul's Cathedral while three quarters of a billion watched on television.

A dashing prince, a bride with a Cinderella story, and the pageantry and pomp of an ancient ruling house: A great royal wedding is a storybook affair. No matter the twists and turns of the marriages that followed, these legendary unions captured hearts around the world

Princess Elizabeth & Philip Mountbatten

NOVEMBER 20, 1947

Standing 9 ft. tall, the wedding cake featured sugar replicas of the royal residences.

Before she became Queen Elizabeth II, of the United Kingdom of Great Britain, Head of the Commonwealth and Defender of the Faith, she was simply "Lilibet," a young girl madly in love. More than half a century ago, the sheltered 21-year-old heir to the British throne wed her distant cousin Philip Mountbatten, a cosmopolitan 26-year-old Royal Navy lieutenant and a royal in his own right. Born Philippos Schleswig-Holstein-Sonderburg-Glucksburg, the nephew of the deposed King of Greece, the groom was far more worldly than his young bride. Although the pair met when the princess was 13, it wasn't until her late teens that Elizabeth developed a crush on her dashing relative, who served in the Pacific during World War II. In 1946 Philip visited Elizabeth at Balmoral, after which she told her father, King George VI, that she intended to marry. The Palace announced an engagement a year later.

The wedding that followed not only lifted the spirits of a war-weary Britain but marked its future Queen's arrival on the world stage. Spectators lined London's streets to catch a glimpse of the bridal route from Buckingham Palace to Westminster Abbey, where the couple exchanged vows before the Archbishop of Canterbury and 2,500 guests. After the ceremony the pair and 150 others dined on a wedding breakfast of fish and partridge at the palace. Philip, who had been given the title Duke of Edinburgh, then cut the wedding cake with his sword and thus began an enduring royal union. Fifty years later, in 1997, the Queen said this of her husband: "He has quite simply been my strength and stay all these years, and I owe him a debt greater than he would ever claim."

A LASTING LOVE
"The Queen's been through wars and the kind of domestic dramas we can only guess at," says royal watcher Judy Wade. "But couples who stay together that long settle down into a kind of glow."

PRINCESS
ELIZABETH &
PHILIP
MOUNTBATTEN

**A WEDDING TO
REMEMBER**
The white horses of
the Household Cavalry
escorted the bride's
carriage through
Trafalgar Square

A PRINCESS BRIDE
"If they had scoured the globe, they could not have found anyone so suited to the part," wedding guest Winston Churchill said of Elizabeth.

THE DRESS

For a dress that would be seen by millions, Elizabeth turned to royal favorite Norman Hartnell, the man who had helped create her mother's trademark style. Reportedly inspired by a floral-themed Botticelli painting, Hartnell worked with 10,000 pearls to embroider the gown in a flower motif. The designer, who also produced the bridesmaids' gowns, used ivory duchess satin for the main dress, along with silk tulle for the 15-ft. train. Teams of seamstresses worked on the dress, which took more than seven weeks to create.

Grace Kelly & Prince Rainier III *of* Monaco

APRIL 19, 1956

I certainly don't think of my life as a fairy tale," Grace Kelly once said. But to the rest of the world, the marriage of one of Hollywood's most beautiful stars to the ruler of a tiny Mediterranean principality was pure enchantment. Prince Rainier III of Monaco was a dapper 31-year-old bachelor when he met the 25-year-old Kelly—fresh from an Oscar win for 1954's *The Country Girl*—during the Cannes Film Festival. Smitten, Rainier kept her in his sights until he received an invitation to her family's Philadelphia home the next year. Two weeks later the couple were engaged. The jaded movie star admitted being swept off her feet. "I barely know him," she confided. "I don't know what will happen."

If their courtship was fast but conventional, the wedding was anything but. Grace and Rainier's 1956 nuptials set the gold standard for royal unions to come: 1,600 journalists and a broadcast to 30 million viewers worldwide. For the Roman Catholic ceremony, the bride glowed in a gown of rose-point lace (see box) at St. Nicholas Cathedral in Monaco. The couple exchanged vows before 1,100 guests, including Hollywood royalty Ava Gardner, Gloria Swanson and Cary Grant. On her honeymoon cruise on the Mediterranean, bridesmaid and fellow actress Rita Gam recalled, Grace wrote her to say "it took her a week to recover from that extraordinary day." Kelly settled into a traditional role as royal consort and became a devoted mother to three children. She died, aged 52, in a car crash in 1982, and Monaco—and its prince—were never the same. Biographer Jeffrey Robinson later asked Rainier about remarrying and was told, "How could I? Everywhere I go, I see Grace."

"I remember her saying, 'I found my prince.'" Kelly's bridesmaid and fellow actress Rita Gam told PEOPLE. "I thought she meant the generic term. Then I found out he really was a prince."

THE PICTURE OF GRACE
Helen Rose (above) and 35 MGM
employees worked for six weeks
to create the dress for Kelly (seen
at right with Rainier at their
reception; the prince designed
his groom's costume himself).

THE DRESS

As a gift to Kelly, MGM directed its wardrobe department to create an ornate bridal gown for the princess-to-be. Led by legendary designer Helen Rose, who had dressed Kelly for films such as *The Swan* and her last feature, *High Society,* Hollywood costumers painstakingly worked with yards of silk gauze and rose-point lace with seed-pearl details to construct the upper portion of the ivory gown. The silk-laden skirt was made of peau de soie, faille and tulle and enhanced by petticoats. Made of silk net, the bride's veil allowed Kelly's face to be visible. To complete the look, Rose added lace and pearl touches to Kelly's prayer book, shoes and headdress. Designs were kept top secret until two days before the ceremony; within hours of the release of sketches, New York garment companies were copying the design. But if her outfit was regal, Kelly walked down the aisle with one humble touch: Hidden inside her left shoe was a single penny for luck.

MAGIC IN MONACO
Grace (with her bridesmaids at her reception) was "a total vision" on her wedding day, recalled her friend Gam. After the civil ceremony, a luncheon was served at the palace. The couple traveled by Rolls from the cathedral to another elaborate reception.

DETAILS *of the* DAY

◆ Before the wedding a 65-member bridal party—and Kelly's black poodle, Oliver—crossed the Atlantic on the ocean liner *Constitution*. To pass the time, the movie star and her friends played shuffleboard and charades. When the ship entered Monaco's harbor, it was greeted by a flotilla of paparazzi, and the prince, who sailed out to meet her.

◆ Mobbed by thousands of well-wishers and journalists, the bride and groom legally wed in a civil ceremony April 18 at the Grimaldi palace. Crews from MGM filmed the service, which had to be reenacted for the cameras.

◆ The following morning the Bishop of Monaco presided over a Roman Catholic wedding mass at St. Nicholas Cathedral in Monte Carlo, which houses the ancestral tombs of the Grimaldi dynasty.

◆ Kelly's six bridesmaids were Rita Gam, high school pal Maree Frisby, college roommate Judith Balaban, drama school friends Sally Parrish and Elizabeth Thompson and modeling friend Carolyn Scott. Her sister Margaret was matron of honor.

◆ Bridesmaids wore yellow organdy dresses, hats and gloves. Flower girls sported dresses from Neiman Marcus and shoes from JCPenney.

◆ The six-tier wedding cake was decorated with miniature Monacan and American flags and topped with a crown.

◆ Gifts included a Rolls-Royce; a gold-and-bone hatchet; and a $224,000 set of diamond earrings, bracelet and necklace from Monaco and Monte Carlo's casino. Director Alfred Hitchcock, who would later make *Psycho,* sent a unique bridal gift: a shower curtain.

◆ For the honeymoon the newlyweds sailed the Mediterranean on Rainier's *Deo Juvante II,* the prince's gift to his bride.

◆ Kelly foreshadowed her own romantic destiny by playing a princess in 1956's *The Swan.*

Lisa Halaby & King Hussein *of* Jordan

JUNE 15, 1978

It may well have been the simplest royal wedding ever," Queen Noor wrote of her 1978 nuptials to Jordan's King Hussein. In fact, the entire ceremony—in which Lisa Halaby, a 26-year-old All-American Princeton grad, became queen of a traditional Muslim society—took less than five minutes. The bride, in a modest Christian Dior white-silk gown, was the only woman present as she exchanged Arabic vows with Hussein in the Oriental sitting room of her mother-in-law's palace. Afterward they joined their families and 500 guests for hors d'oeuvres and Pepsi in the palace garden. Later that day the King proclaimed his bride Queen Noor al-Hussein, the "light of Hussein."

They had seemed an unlikely pair. She was a modern career woman; he, a 42-year-old thrice-married monarch with eight children. But during their brief courtship—they met when Halaby, a budding architect, was working on an airport-design project in Amman—the pair discovered shared passions that included skiing, sailing and Jordan itself. Hussein wasn't opposed to modern romance: He wooed his intended with Abba's song "Take a Chance on Me." Noor embraced her new country, campaigning for women's rights and championing local artists. But family—which included their four children and a pet camel named Fluffy—came first. "He is my life, my love, my career," she once said about her husband. Hussein's death on Feb. 7, 1999 brought their 20-year marriage to an end. But Noor, who now splits her time between Jordan and the U.S., retains a strong connection. Shortly after her husband's death she told a reporter, "We are still making the journey together."

"I see a young woman flushed with optimism and hope," Noor later wrote about her wedding day.

The newlyweds struggled to cut the cake; nobody told them the bottom layer was cardboard.

"I have betrothed myself to thee for the dowry agreed upon," Noor vowed to Hussein before an Islamic sheik. The terms of her royal dowry were not disclosed.

MARRYING INTO ISLAM

"I became a Muslim on the morning of my wedding," Noor wrote in her 2003 autobiography *Leap of Faith*. "We went into the sitting room and I proclaimed the testimony of faith—I declare there is no God but Allah and Muhammad is His messenger." According to Islamic law, Noor was the only woman present at her wedding ceremony, which was attended by close male relatives on both sides. No rings were exchanged; the couple's brief vows were sealed by clasping their hands together. The daughter of a Syrian-American father and Scandinavian mother, who was raised nominally as a Protestant (although she was never baptized), Noor embraced her new religion and celebrated its principles. "Islamic law treats males and females equally," she said during a 2003 lecture. "The oppression of women is not part of Islam but contrary to it."

Lady Diana Spencer & Prince Charles

JULY 29, 1981

I t was, as Archbishop of Canterbury Robert Runcie put it, "the stuff of which fairy tales are made." What's clear is that the wedding of Prince Charles and Lady Diana Spencer transformed the House of Windsor, perhaps the world, forever. At 20, the bride was the epitome of an English rose; her prince, 32, was suave if not handsome. There was a tiara laden with diamonds and even a glass coach. Around the world 750 million watched on TV, and even the jaded were awed. "No Hollywood production could have matched what I saw today," said actor Richard Burton. The pageantry at St. Paul's Cathedral on July 29, 1981, marked the creation not just of a princess but of a superstar. And for a generation of women, the wedding would be a touchstone: What would it have been like to step into Di's embroidered silk slippers that day?

Years later the Princess of Wales herself would expose the dark side of the fairy tale, claiming that even as she walked down the aisle, she knew that Charles had never stopped loving Camilla Parker Bowles, seated among his family and friends. She also would blame the groom and his chilly family for the bulimia that began during their engagement and plagued her for years. (By her wedding day, the waist on Diana's gown had been taken in six inches.)

Somehow, even that harsh reality fails to diminish the romance of the event itself. Many who knew Diana saw only giddiness as she prepared for the moment that Britain would mark with bonfires, fireworks and commemorative bric-a-brac galore. During top-secret fittings for the wedding party at the atelier of designers David and Elizabeth Emanuel, "we used to have a great time,"

BUCKINGHAM PALACE
Though only 20 when she wed a prince 12 years her senior, Lady Diana Spencer did not promise to "obey" him; that traditional vow was omitted at the couple's request.

THE ROYALS

INSIDE THE
PALACE
Royal photographer
Patrick Lichfield noted
that Di "was extremely
quick to comfort"
Clementine Hambro
when she fretted before
a post-nuptial photo
session. She had
taught Hambro, then 5,
in kindergarten.

Sarah-Jane Gaselee, an 11-year-old bridesmaid, later told authors Jayne Fincher and Judy Wade. "She and Charles were really in love as far as I could see. . . . I saw them cuddling on the sofa and during the rehearsals they had their arms linked and they were skipping down the aisle."

Their unlikely courtship had begun a year earlier on a bale of hay in Sussex, where Diana and the prince were guests at a country house. Di, 19, had offered condolences on the death of Charles's great-uncle Lord Mountbatten, prompting him to take a second look at the "jolly" sister of ex-girlfriend Sarah Spencer. Soon the erudite prince was wooing the lightly educated blue blood who had more royal ancestors than the Windsors themselves.

Before an intimate supper at Windsor Castle on Feb. 6, 1981, Charles proposed,

> ## "During the rehearsals [Di and Charles] had their arms linked and they were skipping down the aisle"
>
> — SARAH-JANE GASELEE

and Diana dissolved into giggles. The ring came later: She plucked it from a selection sent by Garrard, the royal jeweler, choosing the $63,000 bauble because "it was the biggest," she once joked.

The Waleses' wedding was destined to be defined by its imperial scale. Gold-embossed invitations went to more than 2,500 guests. By July nearly 6,000 gifts had arrived at St. James's Palace. Among the pile: sapphires from a Saudi prince and a ton of peat from a British district council.

Two nights before the nuptials, Charles and his betrothed gave a ball for 800 friends and family members at Buckingham Palace. Spirits were high: According to Diana's biographer Andrew Morton, "Princess Margaret attached a

ST. PAUL'S CATHEDRAL
After Diana's four-minute walk up the 330-ft. aisle, Charles told her, "You look wonderful." She replied, "Wonderful for you," according to Jayne Fincher and Judy Wade in *Diana: Portrait of a Princess*. Here, the wedding party after the service.

DETAILS *of the* DAY

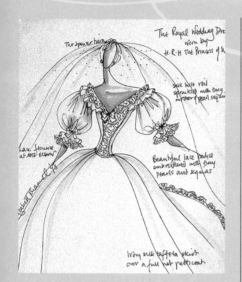

THE BRIDAL GOWN

The design team of Elizabeth and David Emanuel produced at least one backup copy of Diana's crinolined wedding gown, made from 40 yards of silk spun on Britain's only silk farm. "She wanted the dress to be something that people would love to watch," said Elizabeth. Hand-stitched over a three-month period, the dress that Diana wore on her wedding day was trimmed with vintage lace and had a tiny diamond-studded golden horseshoe sewn into the waistband for good luck. After the princess was killed in 1997, the gown was placed on display at a museum at Althorp, her family's estate.

THE FAMILY JEWELS

Along with the Spencer tiara that anchored her veil, Di's borrowed finery included these elegant diamond earrings loaned by her mother, Frances Shand Kydd.

THE WEDDING RECEPTION

Held at Buckingham Palace, the 1 p.m. "breakfast" for about 100 featured lamb, fish and a chicken dish, *Suprème de Volaille Princesse de Galles.* Strawberries and Cornwall cream were served along with champagne. Weighing in at 168 lbs., the wedding cake made by David Avery, a chief cook at the Royal Naval Cookery School, was five tiers of rum-laced fruitcake robed in marzipan and icing.

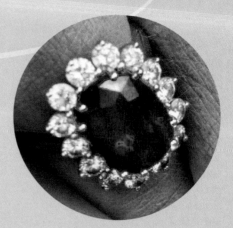

THE RING

One of the most famous (and frequently imitated) baubles worn by a Windsor, the knuckle-dusting engagement ring chosen by Diana—an 18-carat sapphire set in white gold encircled by 14 diamonds—now belongs to her oldest son, Prince William, who asked for it as a keepsake after she died.

THE HONEYMOON

After 2 ½ days at Earl Mountbatten's estate, Broadlands, the newlyweds cruised the Mediterranean on *Britannia.* On Aug. 19 at Balmoral, the cozy-looking pair met the press.

balloon to her tiara; Prince Andrew tied another to the tails of his dinner jacket."

When the wedding day dawned, a million spectators had begun to line the route from the Mall to Ludgate Hill. Inside Clarence House, where Diana and her bridesmaids collected in her dressing room, the bride was "sitting in front of a TV, dressed in her jeans, and the tiara was being put on her head," bridesmaid India Hicks told Fincher. "She started to shoo anyone who got in the way of the TV screen out of the way because, obviously, she was very interested to see [footage about herself] on television. It was all very new and exciting."

"Diana was in her jeans, and the tiara was being put on her head..."

—INDIA HICKS

As it was to the millions of strangers who soaked up every detail from Diana's meringue-confection dress and its 25-ft. train, both wrinkled from the coach ride, to the couple's slight stumbles during their vows. (Diana would pledge herself to "Philip Charles Arthur George," transposing the first two names and prompting Prince Andrew to say with a laugh, "She's married my father.") The groom's grandmum misted up during the ceremony; his mother beamed.

By the time the wedding procession wound back to Buckingham Palace, Diana's charisma had already taken hold. Riding in a 1902 state landau surrounded by cavalrymen, the bridal couple were cheered by pensioners and punk rockers, Yankee tourists and British bobbies. When Charles obeyed the crowd's calls to "kiss her, kiss her" as the two stood on the palace balcony, few could imagine that anything could ever separate the new princess from her prince.

EDWARD VAN CUTSEM

LORD NICHOLAS WINDSOR

SARAH-JANE GASELEE

PRINCE EDWARD

INDIA HICKS

CATHERINE CAMERON

WHERE *are*

PRINCE
ANDREW

LADY SARAH
CHATTO

CLEMENTINE
HAMBRO

they NOW?

Edward van Cutsem
A banker married to heiress Tamara Grosvenor, van Cutsem, 33, is a chum of Prince William's.

Lord Nicholas Windsor
Windsor, 36, has battled depression for years; now a Catholic, he does charity work.

Sarah-Jane Gaselee
Then an 11-year-old whose family knew Prince Charles, Gaselee, 36, is living a quiet life as a mom.

Prince Edward
Formerly a film-company exec, he is now 42 and married to Sophie, Countess of Wessex, and is father of Lady Louise Windsor, 3.

Prince Andrew
Dad to Princesses Beatrice, 18, and Eugenie, 16, the divorced Andrew, 46, has not had a steady girlfriend for several years.

Lady Sarah Chatto
Princess Margaret's child, now 42, wed actor Daniel Chatto in '94; their sons are Samuel, 10, and Arthur, 7.

Catherine Cameron
Charles's goddaughter Cameron, 31, is an assistant at a London literary agency.

India Hicks
Author Hicks, 38, lives in the Bahamas with David Flynt Wood and their sons Conrad, 3, Amory, 7, and Felix, 9.

Clementine Hambro
A kindergarten pupil of Diana's and the youngest bridesmaid, Hambro, 29, is a writer and actress.

Attending the nuptial mass were Britain's Prince Charles, Jordan's Queen Rania and Japan's Prince Naruhito, as well as Placido Domingo and Nelson Mandela

Letizia Ortiz & Felipe *of* Spain

MAY 22, 2004

He was a playboy royal whose globe-trotting past included romances with a German countess and a Norwegian model. She was a TV journalist, the daughter of a newspaperman and a nurse. But when Spain's Crown Prince Felipe wed anchorwoman Letizia Ortiz, their modern love affair took a backseat to tradition. As rain fell on Madrid's Almudena Cathedral, Ortiz, now 31, arrived at her ceremony like a storybook princess, resplendent in a diamond tiara on loan from her mother-in-law-to-be, Queen Sofia. As she walked down the aisle, 1,400 guests craned for a glimpse of the woman who had finally captured the prince's heart. Among those in attendance: members of 30 royal families and 15 heads of state, including Felipe's mother and his father, King Juan Carlos. The solemn ceremony had spontaneous moments: Archbishop Antonio María Rouco Varela dropped a few of the 500-year-old coins he gave Felipe to exchange with Letizia (a custom signifying shared possessions), and Felipe glanced down at crib notes after forgetting some of his vows.

The couple took it all in stride. Meeting at a 2002 dinner party, they began dating the following year, announcing their engagement in November 2003. "How in love I am with Letizia," Felipe, 36, told PEOPLE; Letizia called her intended "an exceptional human being." The public approved: The wedding drew millions of television viewers.

Emerging from the cathedral, the newlyweds climbed into a black vintage Rolls-Royce, which drove along streets adorned with a million geraniums, roses and petunias in Spain's national colors of red and yellow. At their royal palace reception, the couple and guests enjoyed crab-stuffed potato tapas and roasted capon, 1,000 bottles of Spanish sparkling wine and a 6-ft., 370-lb. cake.

Outside the palace, onlookers watched as the elegant couple appeared on a balcony and kissed. Of Letizia, fellow journalist Ana Campillo said, "It's like a fairy tale, not because she is marrying a prince but because she is marrying a man she loves."

Now known as Princess Letizia of Asturias, the former newscaster is the first commoner in line to become Queen of Spain.

Letizia's Valencian silk gown, by designer Manuel Pertegaz, was a hit. Earlier the bride shocked traditionalists by wearing a pantsuit to announce her engagement.

Thousands of Spaniards braved the rain to catch a glimpse of the couple (on the balcony of Madrid's Pardo palace).

Page boys and flower girls wore white-and-gold outfits inspired by 19th-century Goya paintings.

A WORLD *of* ROYAL WEDDINGS

Combining centuries of tradition with modern-day opulence, these royal nuptials captured global attention

GOLDEN COUPLE
The crown prince and Salleh (holding a bouquet of gold and diamonds) exchanged vows atop their thrones during a five-minute traditional Malay ceremony.

More than 100 limousines followed the couple's custom-made gold Rolls-Royce as they drove through the streets of the capital.

In keeping with protocol, more than 2,000 international guests donned white attire to attend the festivities in the royal palace's cavernous Throne Chamber.

CROWN PRINCE AL-MUHTADEE BILLAH BOLKIAH OF BRUNEI & SARAH SALLEH

SEPTEMBER 9, 2004

When it came to the wedding of his oldest son, the Sultan of Brunei spared no expense. Thousands of dignitaries filled a banquet hall in the sultan's 1,788-room palace in the tiny nation's capital, Bandar Seri Begawan, as Prince al-Muhtadee Billah Bolkiah, 30, the Oxford-educated heir to the throne—and a $4.3 billion fortune—wed 17-year-old student Sarah Salleh in a $5 million celebration. Salleh, the daughter of a Swiss nurse and a Bruneian civil servant who met the prince through a friend, arrived an hour late. But the radiant bride did not disappoint her guests. Wearing a diamond tiara and diamond-studded shoes, she was serene as the crown prince gently laid a hand on his wife's head, the only public display of affection between the two. Then the newlyweds bowed and kissed the hands of the Sultan and Queen Saleha (Muhtadee's mother and one of the Sultan's two wives) before greeting a throng waiting just outside the palace gates.

THE WEIGHT OF TRADITION
Masako donned nine kimonos for the 15-minute Shinto wedding ceremony (above) before changing into more Western attire to greet her public (below).

CROWN PRINCE NARUHITO OF JAPAN & MASAKO OWADA

JUNE 9, 1993

After catching the eye of Prince Naruhito at a 1986 palace reception, 29-year-old Masako Owada, a Harvard-educated diplomat, gave up her career to marry into the world's oldest royal family. The thoroughly modern bride rode through Tokyo with her husband after the ceremony—nearly 200,000 cheering spectators lined the streets in support.

The royal couple (above, leaving Kampala's Anglican cathedral with an attendant) wed as men in leopard skins performed ritual dances outside.

Citizens of the East African nation of Uganda longed to witness the splendor of a royal wedding, not to mention seeing their 43-year-old bachelor Kabaka (king) finally married off. Mutebi II, who reigns over the largest of five kingdoms in a country the size of Oregon, granted both these wishes when he wed British public relations executive Sylvia Luswata, 35. The couple, introduced by friends, hosted a lavish palace reception where thousands of guests feasted on 100 roasted cows and gourds of banana beer

PRINCESS PRERNA OF NEPAL & RAJ BAHADUR SINGH

JANUARY 21-22, 2003

When the only daughter of Nepal's King Gyanendra and Queen Komal wed Raj Singh, a 29-year-old computer programmer, there was more than the usual reason to rejoice. About 20 months earlier, the family had suffered tragedy when Princess Prerna's troubled cousin gunned down nine members of the royal family and then committed suicide. The arranged marriage of Prerna, 24, and Singh, a University of California grad, was a festive occasion but a humble affair: The pair wed before just a small group of family and friends. Per Hindu custom, Singh arrived at his bride's home for a traditional ceremony in which the King and Queen showered the couple's hands with water poured from a golden jug and priests chanted and prayed to the elephant god Ganesh. The next day, the couple left Narayanhity Royal Palace for a Kathmandu mansion, ready to start their new life together and put the monarchy's tragic past behind them.

LADY IN RED
Guards carry Princess Prerna (above), in a gold-embroidered sari, to a horse-drawn carriage where her husband awaits. To the strains of pipers playing alongside, the newlyweds were whisked away from the palace to their new home.

The couple first wed behind closed doors in a private ceremony March 21, but posed during the public celebration four months later.

KING MOHAMMED VI OF MOROCCO & SALMA BENNANI

JULY 12-14, 2002

When Morocco's King Mohammed VI wed computer engineer Salma Bennani, he didn't merely break with tradition, he pulverized it. Not only did the monarch forgo an arranged marriage, but for the first time in the history of the kingdom, the royals publicly celebrated a wedding. (The King's own mother's picture had never been officially released, and her marriage wasn't even acknowledged until she had produced a male heir.) In contrast, Mohammed made sure Moroccans feted his 24-year-old bride in a never-before-seen bash, complete with a parade of white-robed servants bearing gifts, dozens of singers and dancers, and international guests including President Clinton, his daughter Chelsea and Jordan's Queen Rania

SPECIAL TRIBUTE
Guests brought gifts
of dates, sandalwood
and perfume in
ornate packages.

THE FANTASIA
Nearly 1,500 riders performed a
popular Moroccan ritual
showcasing horsemanship.

KING LETSIE III OF LESOTHO & KARABO MOTSOENENG

FEBRUARY 18-20, 2000

By tradition, King Letsie, 38, who rules over a landlocked kingdom
the size of Maryland, needed only 40 cows in dowry to gain the hand
of his South African sweetheart, Karabo Motsoeneng, 23. Nonetheless,
for his wedding the King pulled out all the stops. Choirs sang, silver-
helmeted royal horsemen rode by, and hundreds of guests, including
Nelson Mandela, joined the couple for three days of feasting and dancing.

Begun in the 1070s on a rise overlooking the Thames, Windsor sprawls over nearly 13 acres and is the world's largest castle still serving as a royal residence. Queen Elizabeth often weekends there, and the entire royal court joins her in April and June.

BEHIND PALACE WALLS

Every king—and queen—must have a castle. At Windsor the Queen has a dungeon for unruly houseguests, while the Sultan of Brunei's humble home boasts 257 bathrooms. Where would you hang your crown?

THE GREEN DRAWING ROOM
Designed as a library during the reign of Francophile George IV, the room survived the Windsor fire of '92, but its ornate gilded ceiling was badly damaged. It has since been meticulously repaired.

Inside WINDSOR

The Queen's weekend place has all mod cons, plus 650 rooms, 8 thrones and a kitchen that's been cooking since the 11th century

At 900 years and counting, Queen Elizabeth's castle in the Berkshire countryside has seen royal wedding receptions (Prince Charles and Camilla Parker Bowles), burials (the Queen Mum) and parties of note: When Prince William turned 21, an intruder crashed his Africa-themed bash wearing a peach ball gown and a fake beard. Built by William the Conqueror and frequently renovated, the 650-room residence now boasts a dungeon *and* an indoor swimming pool. Seized by Oliver Cromwell during the British Civil War, Windsor suffered another blow in 1992, when a spotlight ignited a curtain in the Private Chapel, sparking a blaze that caused $53 million in damage. Now immaculately restored, the refuge where princesses Elizabeth and Margaret were sent for safety during World War II remains Her Majesty's favorite retreat.

THE CRIMSON DRAWING ROOM
Also designed for George IV, this silk-paneled drawing room was the gathering place for dinner guests during the reign of Queen Victoria.

THE KING'S BEDCHAMBER
Its original occupant was George IV, but in 1855 the room (like others in the castle) was given a makeover to mark the state visit of Napoleon III. After the ruler took his leave, the purple-and-green swags remained on the domed, plumed bed where he had slept.

ST. GEORGE'S HALL
Destroyed by the Great Fire of '92, the Hall, which can accommodate 160 diners, underwent a five-year restoration. In 2004 it was the setting for a state banquet for French President Jacques Chirac.

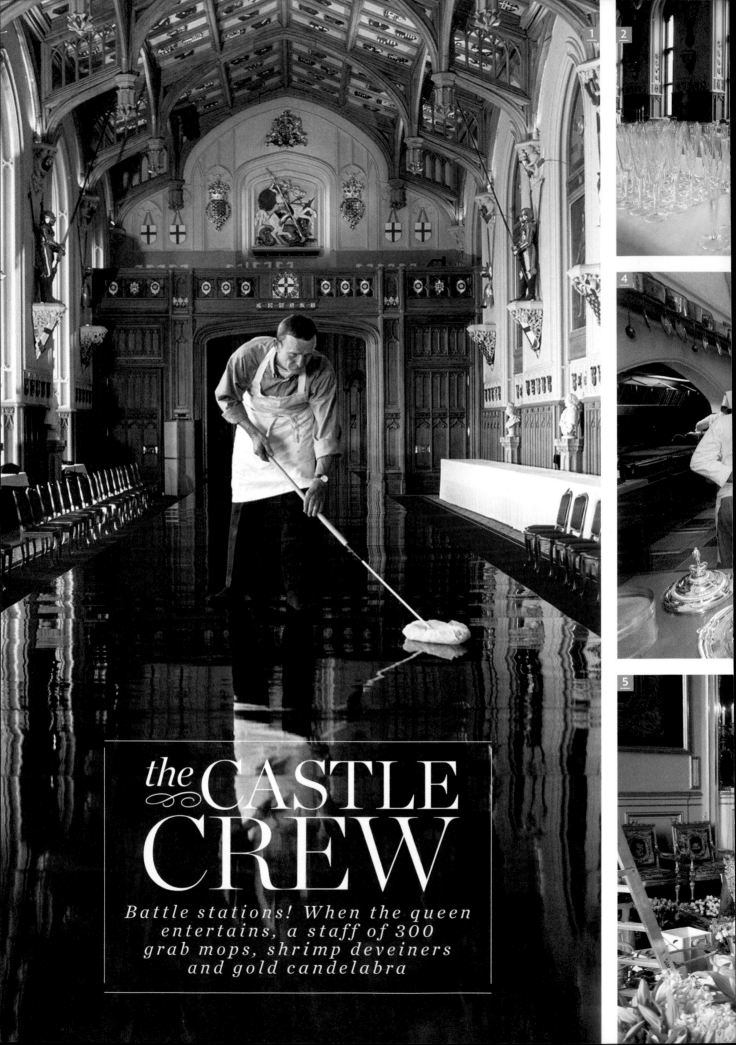

the CASTLE CREW

Battle stations! When the queen entertains, a staff of 300 grab mops, shrimp deveiners and gold candelabra

THE ROYAL TREATMENT

Six months of planning goes into state occasions at Windsor, and household staff are tasked with pulling it off just right. Footmen and underbutlers greet and serve guests, housekeepers unpack and repack their suitcases, and castle "fendersmiths" stoke glowing fireplaces. Who oversees it all? The Queen, who signs off on everything, down to hand soap in the guest rooms. When Her Majesty entertains, spit and polish is all.

1. Castle craftsmen use vinegar and water to clean the Grand Table, used for banquets in St. George's Hall. How to get that gleam? Slide over every inch of the wood in socks.

2. To prepare for 140-guest banquets—which often include champagne, two different dinner wines and a dessert wine—kitchen servants must clean 816 glasses.

3. Flowers are arranged in the gilded Waterloo Chamber, built during George IV's reign.

4. Chefs begin to prep food for banquets 12 hours in advance. The menu, typically three courses, must be approved by the Queen.

5. In the Grand Reception Room, staff assemble some of the thousands of spring blossoms used for Charles and Camilla's '05 wedding.

6. Chief French polisher Eddie Mills arranges a centerpiece among shoulder-high candelabra on the Waterloo Chamber's 50-ft. table. It sits on a carpet reputed to be the largest piece of woven material in the world.

7. Setting the Grand Table requires a ruler to ensure plates, glasses and cutlery (large parties can require more than 900 pieces) are equidistant from each other and the table's edge. Servers are cued by red and green lights flashing from behind a balcony.

BUCKINGHAM: THE

*At her official London address, the Queen
lives it up and gets down to business*

**THE MORNING
COMMUTE**
Her Majesty leaves
Buckingham Palace
in a horse-drawn
carriage for the
traditional opening
of Parliament, as
members of the
Queen's Guard line
the forecourt.
On a typical day,
four sentries stand
watch at the front
of the building.

The Duke of Edinburgh once joked about "living above the shop" in Buckingham Palace. But the royal residence in the British capital—furnished with paintings by Rembrandt and Vermeer, gilded ceilings and grand staircases—is a step above the typical home office. Like every British sovereign since Queen Victoria, the Queen carries out most state duties at the 600-room royal mansion nestled between St. James's Park and Green Park. Once a townhouse built by the Duke of Buckingham in 1702, the palace was expanded to include 240 bedrooms, 78 bathrooms and 92 offices. It now hosts more than 50,000 guests a year at a battery of official receptions. The Queen typically conducts at least 20 royal investitures (the bestowing of knighthoods and other honors) annually in the Ballroom, an expansive space with a 45-ft. ceiling. Other dignitaries are received in the ornate blue-and-gold Music Room, one of 19 state rooms and the site of Prince William's christening. More mundane tasks, such as answering the mail, are confined to the Queen's quarters in the North Wing overlooking Green Park. But life in the palace isn't all work. "I remember rollerblading in the state apartments when they used to take the carpets up, and we used to race round," recalled Prince Andrew, who, along with his siblings Prince Edward and Princess Anne, lives at the palace when he is in the capital. With a staff of more than 400 attending to the royal family's every need, it's no wonder the Duchess of York, Sarah Ferguson, once called Buckingham Palace "the best hotel in London."

WORKING PALACE

A QUEEN'S HOUSEWORK

Though her son Prince Andrew admits trying to get his type-A mum to slow down, telling TIME, "There's no need to do six engagements a day," that doesn't keep Her Majesty from duties that begin at 9:30 each morning and can include meeting with Prime Minister Tony Blair (center, in May 2005) and such dignitaries as the ambassadors for Lesotho (left, in October 2005) and the Kyrgyz Republic (right, in March 2005).

PLAID AND PROUD
The royal family (in 1972, from left: Philip, Elizabeth, Andrew [in blue], Edward, Anne and Charles) show off kilts, some made of Balmoral tartan—designed by Prince Albert in 1853.

BALMORAL | *A Windsor Retreat*

It was a gift from her husband, Prince Albert—though he neglected to wrap it—in 1852, and soon Queen Victoria had dubbed Balmoral, a remote 50,000-acre Scottish estate, "my dear paradise in the highlands." For generations since, usually in summer, the royals have immersed themselves in local culture: donning kilts, downing kippers and eggs and waking each morning to a lone piper playing outside the Queen's bedroom window. Removed from many of their daily duties and the paparazzi, the royals are free to mix with the locals: e.g., playing in cricket matches organized by Prince Edward and showing off their Scottish folk-dancing skills at an annual ball for the estate's workers. Sound like fun? You can do it too. For many years the Queen has rented out several historic cottages on the grounds—some within 300 yards of the castle—for up to $2,000 a week.

HEAVEN IN THE HIGHLANDS
Balmoral's castle and grounds—partially designed by Prince Albert—are open to visitors April through July.

A QUEEN'S BEST FRIENDS
When the Queen (in '72, with her Labs and one of her prized corgis) is at home, she feeds all her many dogs herself—mixing each bowl to specific tastes.

HOME OF THE HIGHLAND FLING

Prince William has often spirited Kate Middleton away to Tom-na-Gaidh—a remote cozy cottage on the grounds. He's hardly the only Windsor to use Balmoral for a romantic getaway. Prince Philip proposed to the Queen at the estate in 1946, and the couple spent part of their honeymoon at Birkhall, a 12-bedroom hunting lodge on the grounds. So did Prince Charles—who called the lodge a "unique haven of coziness and character"—when he wed Camilla, Duchess of Cornwall in 2005.

> "Balmoral is the place where Elizabeth can fulfill her childhood dream of being 'married to a farmer and having lots of horses and cows and dogs'"
>
> —ROYAL BIOGRAPHER SARAH BRADFORD

QUEEN OF ALL SHE SURVEYS
Fifty thousand acres give the
Queen (in '72) plenty of room to
gallop. Filling out the Balmoral
royal pentathlon: salmon fishing,
shooting grouse, running the dogs
and trekking cross-country.

**LIECHTENSTEIN'S
VADUZ CASTLE**
The 800-year-old home
of Liechtenstein's Prince
Hans-Adam sits atop a hill
overlooking the capital of his
tiny country. With a banking
fortune estimated at $4
billion, this monarchy is one
of the world's wealthiest.
That's more than enough
for the Prince to maintain his
storybook home without
opening it to the public.

HOUSE PROUD

A palace in pink, towers fit for Rapunzel, even a throne room of 22-karat gold. When it comes to royal real estate, there's no such thing as excess (or zoning)

THE PALACE OF BRUNEI
The largest residence in the world—completed for $350 million in 1984—boasts 1,788 rooms, including 257 bathrooms. The centerpiece? A vast throne room featuring a wall of 22-karat gold tiles and 12 $1 million crystal chandeliers.

CAMBODIA'S ROYAL PALACE

In the center of Phnom Penh's royal palace complex—begun in 1886 and heavily influenced by the French—lies the main tourist attraction: the Silver Pagoda, with a floor of more than 5,000 silver tiles. Visitors can also admire the palace's plethora of gold and diamond-studded buddhas.

MONACO'S PRINCE'S PALACE

After her 1956 wedding to Prince Rainier III, Princess Grace gave the palace—originally a medieval fortress—a much-needed makeover. First order of business: turning the mustard-yellow outside walls pink. Adjacent to the 225-room palace is a small public zoo started by Rainier, boasting perhaps the world's only royal hippopotamus.

THE ROYAL PALACE OF TONGA

The King of Tonga is famous for his girth—he has weighed in at more than 400 lbs.—but his royal palace, a two-story Victorian home completed in 1867, is more diminutive than most. Still the casual 10-room villa does boast spectacular ocean views.

THE ROYALS

**THE NETHERLANDS'
DRAKENSTEYN CASTLE**
The quirky mansion in the hamlet
of Lage Vuursche became the home
of Princess (now Queen) Beatrix in
1963, and she lived an understated
suburban life there with her family,
often riding a bike around the
countryside. But when she was
crowned Queen in 1980, she traded
up in the real estate department:
she now has two palaces in The
Hague and the huge Royal Palace
in Amsterdam, referred to as the
"eighth wonder of the world" when it
was built between 1648 and 1665.

HER MAJESTY
TRAVELS

Trains, carriages and automobiles: The Queen rides in style

COVERING HER TRACKS

A palace on steel wheels, the Royal Train, used for long journeys within the U.K., has a luxe dining suite and his-and-hers saloons for the Queen and Prince Philip. In a fully equipped office (at left), red boxes contain official documents—the Queen's homework. The yearly operating costs: more than $1.3 million, making it the most expensive form of royal travel.

NOT YOUR TYPICAL HOOD ORNAMENT: The Rover is adorned with a chrome-plated bronze Labrador holding a dead pheasant.

SPIN CONTROL

First ferried in the back of a Land Rover during a 1954 Commonwealth tour, the Queen has stayed loyal to the brand. Since giving Land Rover her royal warrant in 1988, Her Majesty has driven her own SUV, which is fully armored and so comfy that she likes to take in the Windsor horse show from the passenger seat.

GILT TRIP

The most elaborate of all royal coaches, the Gold State Coach, originally built for King George III in 1762, stands 12 feet tall, 24 feet long and weighs 4 tons. Covered with gold leaf and adorned with cherubs, crowns, palm trees and lion heads, the carriage is used when Queen Elizabeth requires a means of transportation unmatched in pomp and pageantry. So far, there have been only three worthy occasions: her 1953 coronation, the Silver Jubilee celebration in 1977 and, most recently, the 2002 Golden Jubilee.

ATIONAL PICTURES
F THE PRINCESS
ND THE PLAYBOY
PAGES 2-7

OVE
f Windsor's
mate cruise

25p

Today's TV: Pages 16 and 17

THE FULL
NCREDIBLE
TORY
e turn
s 15
17

SCANDALS

Heavy lies the head that's hunted by the paparazzi: From the sordid (Fergie's toe-sucking exploits) to the tragic (Princess Grace's car crash) to nearly everything about Diana's long-running tabloid woes and shocking death, the royals have a history of falling hard and fast. And we can't look away

THE OTHER WOMAN
Diana (during a tense meeting with Parker Bowles in 1980) nicknamed her rival the Rottweiler, while Camilla reportedly referred to the princess as "that ridiculous creature."

Sex, lies and secrets made for an unhappily-ever-after ending for Charles and Diana

THE WAR
OF THE WALESES

THE MAJOR
James Hewitt (with Di and Prince William in '91) went on to write a tell-all about their affair.

By October 1991 the Prince and Princess of Wales were deeply unhappy, gazing at the world from a prison of a marriage that had begun, in the words of Diana, with "tremendous hopes in my heart." During a visit to Toronto that month, even strangers could tell that hope was gone: The Waleses' 10-year union had dissolved under the weight of betrayal. So plain was their misery, and so scandalous were the revelations of the following year—Andrew Morton's as-told-to biography about the princess, *Diana: Her True Story,* and transcripts of the pair's adulterous phone conversations among them—that Prime Minister John Major's December 1992 announcement of a royal separation was anticlimactic. But unlike celebrity couples with publicists to curb their worst impulses, Diana and Charles floated damning stories about one another even after they parted. Only Diana's death in Paris with divorced playboy Dodi Fayed brought a lasting truce.

By then the world knew the Waleses' happily-ever-after marriage had actually been an unmitigated disaster. The Windsors quickly discovered that Charles's bride was impossible to control. Diana, in turn, found she had married into a kind of Stepford Kingdom. When Diana confronted Charles on their honeymoon about his relationship with longtime love Camilla Parker Bowles, she was stonewalled.

DIANA
Her True Story

DI STRIKES BACK
Andrew Morton's 1992 biography *Diana: Her True Story* (left) rocked the Windsors' world with revelations—supplied by Diana herself—of bulimia, suicide attempts and Prince Charles's infidelity. In a tearful 1995 BBC interview (below), she confessed her own infidelity and determination to become "queen of people's hearts." Right: In 1997 Di and Dodi Fayed vacationed in Saint-Tropez just nine days before their fatal crash.

Distraught, the 20-year-old battled an eating disorder, losing so much weight after the 1982 birth of Prince William that courtiers questioned her sanity. Depending on whom you believe, Charles and Camilla resumed their affair right after his wedding or waited until his marriage was "irretrievably broken," as the prince said in a 1994 BBC interview. That broadcast contained another revelation: that he had never loved his princess bride. Diana fired back with a TV tell-all of her own a year later, confiding to journalist Martin Bashir, "There were three of us in this marriage, so it was a bit crowded."

The Waleses' troubles first came to light in October 1987, after the couple had spent 37 consecutive days apart. "Palace flaks can put forth as many excuses as they want," an insider told PEOPLE. "The prince and princess are leading separate lives." By then, Diana was seeking comfort outside her marriage, eventually being linked to bodyguard Barry Manakee, banker Philip Dunne, car salesman James Gilbey, army major James Hewitt, art dealer Oliver Hoare, rugby player Will Carling and surgeon Hasnat Khan. Hewitt, a riding instructor, later traded on his notoriety with a tell-all book that earned

him the nickname Major Rat; a recorded cell phone chat between Diana and Gilbey revealed his nickname for the princess—"Squidgy"—to the world. Charles and Camilla were likewise embarrassed by a salacious cell phone transcript, but "the drip, drip effect of embarrassing revelations about [Diana's] private life had a corrosive effect on her public image," said Patrick Jephson, her chief of staff.

When the Waleses divorced in 1996, Diana was stripped of the title Her Royal Highness but at last free to forge her own path, devoting herself to charity and outshining her former in-laws in the process. By 1997 it seemed that both she and Charles were ready to bury the hatchet. Finally able to acknowledge Camilla, he was magnanimous when pictures of Diana embracing Fayed, heir to the owner of Harrods, hit the tabs that August. "I'm happy if she's happy," he told a reporter. But Di's happiness was cut brutally short. And the Prince of Wales, his second wife and the monarchy itself are still recovering from years of bad press. At least one question remains: How could Charles and Diana, the golden couple blessed with everything, have wasted so much time making each other miserable?

THE DEATH OF A PRINCESS

On Aug. 31, 1997, a vacationing Diana and Dodi Fayed left the Paris Ritz in a Mercedes S280 at 12:20 a.m. with bodyguard Trevor Rees-Jones and driver Henri Paul. The group was pursued by paparazzi in a 90-mph car chase. Nine years on, the crash in the Place de l'Alma tunnel that killed Diana, Dodi and Paul remains shrouded in mystery. A $3.5 million investigation that has delved into the incident—including murder rumors—seems likely to confirm it was an accident. But one thing is certain: Even in death, Diana continues to make headlines

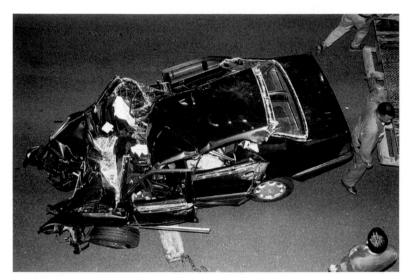

MOURNING THE QUEEN OF HEARTS
After Diana's Paris car crash (left), thousands flocked to Buckingham Palace to mourn her death. The Queen, on vacation at Balmoral, drew sharp criticism for remaining in Scotland rather than joining the throngs paying their respects in London.

A TENSE FAMILY FUNERAL
In a eulogy that enraged the Windsors, Di's brother Charles Spencer (walking in her Sept. 6 funeral with, from left, Princes Philip, William, Harry and Charles) said of her sons, "We will not allow them to suffer the anguish that used regularly to drive you to tearful despair."

ROYAL MISTRESS, PART 1

As icebreakers go, this one is a doozy: Upon meeting Prince Charles at a party in 1972, Camilla Parker Bowles famously declared, "My great-grandmother was the mistress of your great-great-grandfather. I feel we have something in common." Indeed, her great-grandmother Alice Keppel had been the love of King Edward VII's life, although both were otherwise married. So openly acknowledged was the relationship that Queen Alexandra invited Keppel to the King's bedside when he was dying in 1910. "A royal mistress," Keppel is reported to have said—flaunting a sassy streak not unlike her great-granddaughter's—"should curtsy first, then leap into bed."

Camilla (with Charles at their April 9, 2005, Windsor wedding) is a descendant of royal mistress Alice Keppel. After her wedding, Camilla had the right to the title Princess of Wales, but perhaps because of its link to Diana chose to be called the Duchess of Cornwall instead.

THE TROUBLE WITH HARRY

His big brother is cautious, deliberate and ever-responsible. Prince Harry? He's working on it. At 16, the party prince made news for underage drinking and pot smoking, prompting his father to send Harry for a day visit to a London drug rehab clinic for a dose of reality. Among his favorite places to party at the time: "Club H," the young princes' basement rec room, outfitted with a fully stocked bar, at the royal family's Highgrove estate. Then, in 2005, the prince—whom Princess Diana once playfully called "the naughty one"—managed to offend just about everyone when he turned up at a friend's costume party dressed as a Nazi soldier, complete with a swastika armband. "I am very sorry if I caused any offense," he said in a statement. "It was a poor choice of costume."

YES SHE CAN-CAN
Fergie (wrestling with
her dress in '88) left
her marriage millions
of dollars in debt.
"I was needy and full
of doubts," she said
of her affair with
Bryan (right).

THE Sun

Thursday, August 20, 1992   25p   Today's TV: Pages 22 and 23

25p
We're toupee cheaper
AND you get a free
syrup–Turn to Page 9

FERGIE TOE-JOB

¡HOLA!

Too much . . . millionaire Bryan kisses Fergie's foot as the fun-loving Duchess sprawls on a lounger at their St Tropez villa

**Picture will make
her Royal outcast**

WORLD PHOTO SENSATION

FERGIE'S FOLLIES

*She was fun
and frisky. But
merry wife of
Windsor Sarah
Ferguson had
a knack for
making messes*

Gullible and naive" by her
own description, Sarah Ferguson wrote
in her 1996 autobiography that she "was
never cut out for the job" of being royal.
The feisty 26-year-old redhead was
hailed as a breath of fresh air when she
wed Prince Andrew in 1986, but soon
drew criticism for everything from her
weight ("Duchess of Pork," sneered Fleet
Street) to her clothes to her mothering
skills, which came under fire when she
left 6-week-old daughter Beatrice to join
Andrew in Australia. Then came rumors
of strife in the royal marriage, beginning
with Fergie's alleged affair with Texas
businessman Steve Wyatt in 1989. Her
troubles reached a low in 1992, when the
duchess—then separated from her husband—was photographed topless on the
Côte d'Azur while American financial
adviser John Bryan (a distant cousin of
Wyatt's) sucked her toes. The photos
made headlines, and "the Queen was
furious," wrote Fergie. In 1996 she and
Andrew divorced. Still close to her ex, she
found a second act as a pitchwoman for
Weight Watchers in the U.S. "The harder
I pushed," she said of her Windsor years,
"the more things fell apart."

INSTRUMENT OF ABDICATION

I, Edward the Eighth, of Great Britain, Ireland, and the British Dominions beyond the Seas, King, Emperor of India, do hereby declare My irrevocable determination to renounce the Throne for Myself and for My descendants, and My desire that effect should be given to this Instrument of Abdication immediately.

In token whereof I have hereunto set My hand this tenth day of December, nineteen hundred and thirty six, in the presence of the witnesses whose signatures are subscribed.

SIGNED AT
FORT BELVEDERE
IN THE PRESENCE
OF

A HISTORIC CHOICE
"I have found it impossible to carry the heavy burden of responsibility and to discharge my duties of King as I would wish to do," Edward said in a 1936 radio broadcast that reached millions, "without the help and support of the woman I love."

THE KING AND MRS. SIMPSON
EVENING STANDARD

FOR THE WOMAN HE LOVED

He was the heir to the British throne; she was a twice-divorced American socialite. Who would have guessed that the 1930 meeting of the future King Edward VIII, then 36, and ambitious Wallis Simpson, 34, at a house party would change history? But so besotted was Edward that in 1936, after just 325 days on the throne, he sacrificed a kingdom to marry the woman he couldn't resist. (The King was head of the Church of England, which didn't allow marriage to a divorced person.) After refusing his family's pleas to abandon Wallis, Edward passed the throne to his brother George VI and wed Simpson in 1937. "She promised to bring into my life something that wasn't there," he wrote in his 1951 autobiography. "I was convinced that with her I'd be a more creative and more useful person." The royal family snubbed Simpson as a social climber but received her at her husband's funeral in 1972, and again in '86 at her own.

Margaret (in 1947) was forced to keep Townsend (left) at a distance.

MARGARET'S FORBIDDEN LOVE

It was the lint that launched a thousand headlines: At her sister Elizabeth's 1953 coronation, Princess Margaret brushed a bit of fuzz off the uniform of Group Capt. Peter Townsend. The intimate flick exposed a secret: The princess, 22, and Townsend, 38 and a divorced father, were having an affair. His divorce made him unsuitable in the eyes of the Church of England, and Margaret ultimately bowed to intense religious and political pressures and ended the liaison in 1955. Years later, said her friend Lady Glenconner, Margaret sometimes wondered "what her life would have been like if they had married."

THE NAZI CONNECTION

Living in exile in France, Edward and his bride—then Duke and Duchess of Windsor—embarrassed Britain by visiting Hitler in 1937 (right). With the royal family's German roots already a source of suspicion, many feared the pair were Nazi sympathizers plotting to restore Edward to the throne. Such suspicions were never firmly proved, but Allied intelligence did spy on the couple, and the British government sent them off to the Bahamas during World War II

Daily Mirror

MARGARET DECIDES:

DUTY BEFORE LOVE

PRINCESS MARGARET, in this dramatic announcement from Clarence House last night, told the world that she had renounced the love of Group Captain Peter Townsend.

"I would like it to be known that I have decided not to marry Group Captain Peter Townsend. I have been aware that, subject to my renouncing my rights of succession, it might have been possible for me to contract a civil marriage. But, mindful of the Church's teaching that Christian marriage is indissoluble, and conscious of my duty to the Commonwealth, I have resolved to put these considerations before any others. I have reached this decision entirely alone, and in doing so I have been strengthened by the unfailing support and devotion of Group Captain Townsend. I am deeply grateful for the concern of all those who have constantly prayed for my happiness.

(Signed) Margaret."

Peter Townsend leaves—alone   SEE BACK PAGE

THE TROUBLED

DEATH ON THE ROAD
The fatal crash was in France, just outside Monaco's borders. Below: Stephanie sustained a fractured vertebra and was unable to leave her bed to attend Grace's funeral.

THE DEATH OF PRINCESS GRACE

From Philadelphia debutante to Hollywood star to leading lady of Monaco, Princess Grace lived a life that was nothing less than cinematic. So it's not surprising that her tragic death at 52 seemed like something out of the movies. On Sept. 13, 1982, Grace and her then-17-year-old daughter, Princess Stephanie, were driving on a road near Monaco when their Rover plunged 120 feet down a steep mountainside. Grace died the next day; almost immediately rumors swirled that Stephanie—who was below legal driving age—had been at the wheel and that the palace had covered up the truth in order to protect her. Doctors later reported that Kelly suffered two strokes, and in 2002 Stephanie told her side of the story for the first time to *Paris Match*. "I wasn't driving," she said. "I tried everything [to stop it]." She acknowledged that she had climbed out of the driver's side window, which made some think she had been driving: "The passenger's side was crushed." Of the rumors, she said, "I can't stand it anymore. Let my mother rest in peace, and as for me, let me live."

HOUSE *of* GRIMALDI

Albert admitted fathering Jazmin (left, with Rotolo) and Alexandre (with Coste).

PRINCE ALBERT: MISADVENTURES IN FATHERHOOD

Monaco's bachelor prince has a playboy reputation. But even jaded Grimaldi watchers were shocked in 2005 when Prince Albert, 48, admitted to fathering a son, Alexandre Eric Stéphane, 3, with flight attendant Nicole Coste. Just 11 months later, he acknowledged paternity of 14-year-old Jazmin Grace Grimaldi, who lives with her mother, ex-waitress Tamara Rotolo, in Palm Desert, Calif. Neither child is qualified to inherit the crown, but both stand to collect a share of Albert's $2 billion fortune.

Rob Lowe   Mario Jutard   Daniel Ducruet   Raymond Gottlieb   Franco Knie   Adans Lopes Peres   Franck Brasseur

THE PRINCESS AND HER MEN

Grace and Rainier's youngest has always been a royal Wild Child. A former swimsuit designer, perfume peddler and pop singer (she released her debut album in '86 and in '91 sang with Michael Jackson on "In the Closet"), she has had a love life that is the stuff of soap operas. Among her exes: Rob Lowe (whom she dated in '86), racecar driver Paul Belmondo, record producer Ron Bloom and businessman Jean-Yves Le Fur. A '95 marriage to bodyguard Daniel Ducruet (father to Louis, 13, and Pauline, 12) ended when he was photographed romping with an ex-Miss Bare Breasts of Belgium. Stephanie then had another child, Camille, in 1998, allegedly with bodyguard Jean-Raymond Gottlieb. (She has never publicly identified the father.) Then it was off to the circus: She toured with elephant tamer Franco Knie (they lived in his trailer), then wed trapeze artist Adans Lopes Peres in 2003. They divorced a year later.

DOING IT HER WAY
"If I shock people," Stephanie (modeling in 1985) once said, "tough luck."

SURF'S UP!
Prince William took a break from his studies at the University of St. Andrews in October 2004 to hit the North Sea surf with pals.

ROYALS *at* PLAY

Norway's Prince Haakon sails on a 264-ft. yacht. William and Harry are always up for a chukker of polo. And Monaco's Grimaldis know all the best beaches. When it comes to fun, there's nothing like the royal treatment

DENMARK
Called the "Love Boat," the 257-ft. *Dannebrog* boasts a smoking salon and piano lounge and is a favorite getaway for Crown Prince Frederik and his Australian bride, Princess Mary (above). Its reputation for romance comes from hosting honeymoons, including that of Frederik's mother, Queen Margrethe, who, declaring herself too in love to eat, barely touched the menu during her cruise with husband Prince Henrik.

my KINGDOM FOR *a* YACHT

With sumptuous suites and 50-man crews on 24-hour call, royal ships sail in deluxe style

NORWAY
Like his parents, King Harald V and Queen Sonja, Norway's Crown Prince Haakon sailed off on the 264-ft. *Norge*—given to the royals by Norwegians in 1947—for his '01 honeymoon with bride Mette-Marit Tjessem (right). Once owned by English millionaire adventurer Sir Thomas Sopwith, the 69-year-old vessel requires a crew of 54 and is most often used for jaunts through Norway's fjords.

MONACO
Prince Rainier and Princess Grace received the 147-ft. *Deo Juvante II*, equipped with four double suites and a deluxe galley, as a wedding gift from Aristotle Onassis. But the couple (with Albert, Caroline and Stephanie in 1972) also loved to cruise in smaller boats.

SPAIN
The Spanish royals traded in their old yacht, after a series of breakdowns at sea, for the 138-ft., $17 million *Fortuna*, which boasts seven deluxe cabins and linens monogrammed with the royal crest. Best of all, the vessel was free—a gift from Spanish businessmen.

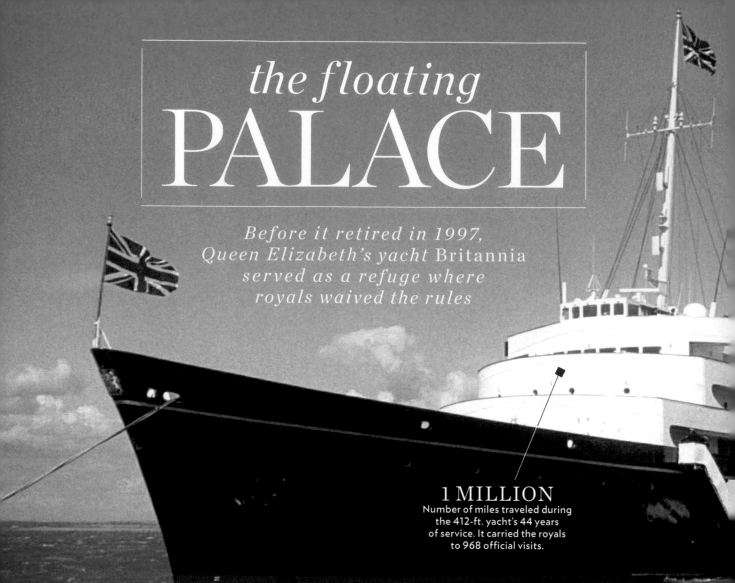

the floating
PALACE

Before it retired in 1997,
Queen Elizabeth's yacht Britannia
served as a refuge where
royals waived the rules

1 MILLION
Number of miles traveled during
the 412-ft. yacht's 44 years
of service. It carried the royals
to 968 official visits.

NEWLYWEDS SET SAIL
Honeymooners Charles and Diana boarded the *Britannia*
during their 1981 trip, for which the prince requested
the yacht's first-ever double bed. Diana spent the
Mediterranean voyage sunbathing on the veranda deck,
while Charles immersed himself in reading. Years later,
when the couple brought young Will and Harry aboard, a
sailor was assigned to keep watch over them.

THE QUEEN'S SPARTAN CABIN
Marked by plain furnishings and single beds, the
royal suites were utilitarian compared with public
areas on board. A door connected the Queen's
bedroom (below) to Prince Philip's quarters.

THE QUEEN WALKS THE PLANK

On her many voyages aboard the *Britannia*, Queen Elizabeth brought along 5 tons of luggage, including her Rolls-Royce (above left) and bottles of Malvern water for tea. Accompanying her were 45 palace household staff and 220 yachtsmen. When upkeep costs forced the yacht out of commission in 1997, an emotional Queen said, "It is with great sadness that we must now say goodbye to *Britannia*."

LUXURY AT SEA

The dining room (above) seats more than 50 guests and has entertained Nelson Mandela and Bill Clinton. The drawing room (left) holds a piano that was frequently played by Princess Diana. One of the Queen's favorite spots? The sun lounge, with its panoramic ocean views. The yacht's most priceless feature was privacy: "It was a haven," says royal photographer Dave Morris. "The Queen could walk around in slacks and a head scarf, and the others would flop around on deck."

Mountain
MAJESTY

When royals hit the slopes, they leave protocol behind

Sarah Ferguson and her daughters princesses Beatrice (left) and Eugenie (right) enjoyed their annual pilgrimage to Verbier in 2004.

For as long as the Swiss Alps have been a destination for the jet set, the world's royals have been enjoying the snow. Klosters, an exclusive resort in eastern Switzerland, has long been favored by the Windsors. "I love the place," said Prince Charles, who has vacationed there since 1978. (A cable car there is named after him.) His brother Prince Andrew and his ex, Sarah Ferguson, prefer to ski in the French-speaking resort of Verbier. As new faces appear in royal circles, so they do on the trails: Prince William's girlfriend, Kate Middleton, attended Charles's pre-wedding ski party at Klosters' Hotel Walserhof in '05

Switzerland, which has no king, imports bluebloods during ski season: In the late '30s, Greek princess Aspasia (far left) headed for the hills with daughter Alexandra (right) and posh pals. Other regal lovers of the local pistes: Monaco's Princess Caroline and Japan's Crown Princess Masako.

Feeding each other's need for speed, princes William, Charles and Harry spent eight-hour days on Canada's Whistler Mountain (on a rare break from Klosters) in '98. The trio also indulged in the odd snowball fight.

SPORT *of* KINGS & QUEENS

Fast, beautiful and expensive, Thoroughbreds are a royal obsession

In her teens Charlotte Casiraghi participated in equestrian events, including a jumping competition in Boulogne, France, in 2004.

Whether riding to hounds or swinging a polo mallet, the royal passion for equestrian sports links the generations. When Elizabeth II was growing up, she bonded with the Queen Mum at the races, and the Windsor men share a passion for polo (some of the royal family's ponies cost $80,000 and hail from as far away as Argentina). And it's not just the Brits who love their equines. The Sultan of Brunei, a riding enthusiast, has owned as many as 200 polo ponies, and he's taken many with him on Royal Brunei Airlines. And in Monaco, Princess Caroline passed her love on to her daughter Charlotte Casiraghi, who began competing in horse shows at age 11

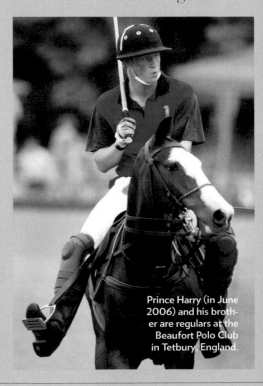

Prince Harry (in June 2006) and his brother are regulars at the Beaufort Polo Club in Tetbury, England.

THE PRINCES AND POLO

For Windsor men, polo—a sport of Persian ancestry that the British cavalry picked up in India in the 19th century—is in the blood. So devoted was Prince Charles—who at one point owned 16 polo ponies—that he endured recurrent back pain, a broken arm and being knocked unconscious after he was thrown from his horse in 2001 before sadly announcing his retirement from the sport in 2005. Now Princes William and Harry are bringing new attention and glamour to the ancient game, playing in charity matches as did their dad (Charles raised an estimated $20 million playing in polo benefits) and showing up with their sporty girlfriends in tow.

Goal! Prince William played for a team sponsored by Thailand in a Surrey, England, charity polo match in June 2005.

In 1980, Princess Margaret held court on Mustique, a Caribbean island where she built a six-bedroom retreat on a 10-acre plot she received as a wedding present.

On Necker Island, the private preserve of Virgin mogul Richard Branson, a young Harry (right) shovels sand on his royal mom during a vacation with William (behind Diana's mother, Frances Shand Kydd) on a 1990 holiday.

SUN KINGS

Up and a wake: On the Med or in Mustique,
royals rule the beach

Princess Caroline's younger son, Pierre, wakeboards in Monaco in 2005.

Showing off her family's good looks and a vast wardrobe of bikinis, Charlotte Casiraghi (in 2001) frequents Monaco's most exclusive beach clubs.

In 2006, Prince William took a flying leap from a yacht off Mustique during a vacation with Kate Middleton. The ultra-chic 1,400-acre island is also a favorite escape for Tom Hanks, Hugh Grant, Denzel Washington and Mick Jagger.

She may be a commoner, but Kate Middleton (who stayed with Will at Mustique's $14,000-a-week Villa Hibiscus resort in May '06) is learning to vacation like a royal.

When temperatures rise, royals escape to the world's swankiest sand. For the Grimaldis, it's their front yard, while Mustique, Barbuda and Necker have long been Windsor ports of call. The Queen may prefer drafty Windsor, but William and Harry hit deluxe Indian Ocean retreats. There will always be an England, but these boys like the beach

THE LITTLE PRINCES
Harry looked up to big brother William during his first day at London's Wetherby School in September 1989.

THE NEXT GENERATION

Growing up royal has perks: your choice of polo ponies, castles to play in, allowances to die for. While their parents struggled to fit into a modern world, the young Windsors and Grimaldis thrive in it. Will they avoid the mistakes of their elders? Time will tell

Charlotte spends her days shopping in Paris boutiques, sipping cappuccinos in Monte-Carlo cafes and playing the piano. Family friend Karl Lagerfeld has compared her to Brigitte Bardot and supplies her with his latest creations.

The Young GRIMALDIS

Grace's grandchildren make Monaco a glamour superpower

Caroline's younger son, Pierre, "likes to joke around," said one of his friends, "to make others laugh."

Can elegance be in your DNA? The coming-of-age of Princess Caroline's children suggests the answer may be *oui*. Raised in rural Provence after their father, Stefano Casiraghi, died in a speed-boat crash in 1990, the trio have taken to the limelight with ease. Chic Charlotte, 20, loves couture and horseback riding; suave Andrea, 21, already has a rep as a ladies' man. Natural comedian Pierre, 19, bends it like Beckham on the soccer field. Friends say they are *nice* too. "They don't act like royalty," says one. "They're just ordinary." But with, perhaps, a hefty helping of je ne sais quoi

The second in line to Monaco's throne, Andrea is called a "heartbreaker" by a friend. A fan of African music, he's often spied in Paris nightclubs in the wee hours. But the chain-smoking hedonist is also a jock, keeping fit by running and windsurfing.

"He has the good fortune not to look like me," Prince Charles said of his infant son (in 1983 at Kensington Palace). Dubbed "Wills" by Princess Diana and "Willie the Wombat" by his father, he also had a dark side, earning the nickname William the Terrible for his tantrums.

WILLIAM

The 41-gun salute that rang out across London on June 21, 1982, heralded a new baby and a new era. Prince William Arthur Philip Louis is the first in his family to be born in a hospital, attend nursery school and graduate from university with honors. If his role made him different (he was assigned a cook, maid and nanny at birth), William was grounded by Diana, who took him to movies and amusement parks like other kids. "I had such a normal childhood," he later said. That left the royal heir with an invaluable asset for any king-to-be: the common touch

The young prince (at a riding competition in 1989) showed early signs of the royal family's love of horses and hunting.

Prince Charming: All smiles at Eton as he strolled with his classmates in 1995, 13-year-old Wills achieved pinup status when he reached adolescence.

By 15 (during a visit to Balmoral), William seemed to exhibit both his father's sense of duty and his mother's effervescent smile.

William showed off his sporting prowess by captaining a team during a soccer match between Eton houses in 2000. He also excelled at water polo and rugby.

All smiles during a stint working with kids in Chile in 2001, in his preuniversity "gap year" William also spent time as a farmhand and training with the Welsh Guards before heading to St. Andrews University.

Though he once said, "I don't want to get married until I'm at least 28," William has dated Kate Middleton (at a polo match in June 2006) since the pair shared an apartment together in college.

William took a break from studying geography at St. Andrews to go fox hunting in November 2002.

Having carried out official duties since he was a teen, Wills joined the Queen at the 2003 Trooping the Colour, a parade marking Her Majesty's birthday.

A PRINCE'S PROGRESS

When asked as a student at St. Andrews University if he wanted to be King, William didn't miss a beat: "It's not a question of wanting to be; it's my duty." Since his '05 graduation, the prince has stepped confidently into adulthood, seemingly unruffled by all the fuss about his future. "Sometimes I do get anxious about it," he has said. "But I don't really worry a lot"

"He's very protective toward me," William has said of Charles. Father and son shared a laugh on a Klosters ski holiday in 2004.

MAMA'S BOY
The little prince (with Diana in Palma de Mallorca, Spain) cuddled with his mother every chance he got.

An army buff at 9, Harry got a taste of military life during a 1993 visit to a British army base in Germany.

HARRY

His full name may be Henry Charles Albert David. But since his 1984 birth, he's been known as Harry, a name that fits. At first, Diana's younger was the shier of her boys. But as he grew, Harry seems to have inherited her high spirits. Molded by Eton and Sandhurst, he's grown into a confident young man who revels in the role of second son. Mother would probably approve. "Royal firstborns may get all the glory," said Diana. "Secondborns enjoy more freedom"

By the time he was 6, Harry (left, with classmates at London's Wetherby School) was marching to his own drummer. Doted on by both parents, he grew even closer to his father (sledding with Harry in the Alps in 1997) after Diana's death.

At Eton, Harry (in his room in 2003) preferred rugby and other sports to homework but nurtured an interest in art.

Goal! Harry displayed his love of soccer during a visit to London's Upton Park, home of West Ham United Football Club, in 2002.

"I just think [my mom would] want us to do this, me and my brother," said Harry of his charity work with AIDS orphans in Lesotho. "I want to try and carry it on to make her proud."

PRINCE OF HEARTS

William may stand to inherit the throne, but his kid brother has no problem grabbing the spotlight. The Windsor family flirt turns 22 in September 2006, and he's already well known as a jock, loyal friend and die-hard man-about-town. He may be reckless, but who can fault his verve? "He skis like he plays polo," observes a pal, "very daringly." Still, there's another side to the Party Prince, an activist who friends say inherited his mother's charisma. But make no mistake, says *Majesty* magazine editor Ingrid Seward. Harry "is going to be the fun one; he'll give us the headlines"

After graduating from Sandhurst in April 2006, Harry (above, in 2005) has continued his military training with an elite British Army regiment. An avid horseman, he spends hours playing polo near his father's Highgrove estate.

HARRY AND CHELSY
Like Harry, whom she's dated for two years, Zimbabwean heiress Chelsy Davy (in South Africa in '06) is known for her zest for life.

FACING THE FUTURE
With a sense of duty—and fun—
not to mention the adoration of
millions, the princes (celebrating
the Queen's birthday in '03) seem
destined to leave their own mark
on the monarchy.

"We've been brought up in different times. The world is changing, as everyone knows. We've changed with it"

—PRINCE HARRY

CREDITS

Editor J.D. Heyman
Creative Directors Philip Bratter,
Rina Migliaccio
Art Director David Jaenisch
Senior Editor Nancy Jeffrey
Picture Editor James Miller
Designers Heath Brockwell, Jorge Colombo
London Bureau Chief Simon Perry
Chief of Reporters Mary Hart
Writers Olivia Abel, Laura Downey, Michelle
Green, Molly Lopez, Ericka Souter, Michelle
Tauber, Ashley N. Williams, Jennifer Wren
Writer-Reporters Greg Adkins, David Cobb
Craig, Marisa Wong
Reporters Rennie Dyball, Deirdre Gallagher,
Kristen Mascia, Hugh McCarten, Lesley Messer,
John Perra, Beth Perry, Ellen Shapiro, Brooke
Bizzell Stachyra, Charlotte Triggs, Melody Wells
Correspondents Karen Nickel Anhalt, Aisha
Labi, Peter Mikelbank, Courtney Rubin,
Monique Jessen
Photo Researchers Elaine Sutton, Su Smith,
Kristy Jell (London), Marie Monteleone
Photo Assistant Florence Nash
Copy Editors Lance Kaplan, Alan Levine
Production Artists Michael Aponte,
Denise Doran, Ivy Lee, Michelle Lockhart,
Cynthia Miele, Daniel Neuburger, Ben Zapp
Scanners Brien Foy, Stephen Pabarue
Administrative Assistant Danielle Cruz
Interns Rebecca Ruiz, Danielle Toth
Special thanks to Robert Britton, David Barbee,
Jane Bealer, Sal Covarrubias, Margery Frohlinger,
Charles Nelson, Ean Sheehy, Jack Styczynski,
Celine Wojtala, Patrick Yang

TIME INC. HOME ENTERTAINMENT
Publisher Richard Fraiman
Executive Director, Marketing Services
Carol Pittard
Director, Retail & Special Sales Tom Mifsud
Marketing Director, Branded Businesses
Swati Rao
Director, New Product Development
Peter Harper
Financial Director Steven Sandonato
Assistant General Counsel
Dasha Smith Dwin
Marketing Manager Laura Adam
Book Production Manager Suzanne Janso
Design & Prepress Manager
Anne-Michelle Gallero
Special thanks to Bozena Bannett,
Alexandra Bliss, Glenn Buonocore, Robert
Marasco, Brooke McGuire, Jonathan
Polsky, Chavaughn Raines, Mary Sarro-Waite,
Ilene Schreider, Adriana Tierno

Copyright © 2007 Time Inc. Home
Entertainment. Published by People Books,
Time Inc., 1271 Avenue of the Americas, New
York, NY 10020. All rights reserved. No part of
this book may be reproduced in any form or by
any electronic or mechanical means, including
information storage and retrieval systems,
without permission in writing from the publisher,
except by a reviewer, who may quote brief
passages in a review.

ISBN10:1-933821-37-X, ISBN 13:978-1-933821-37-5
Library of Congress Control Number: 2006939690
People Books is a trademark of Time Inc. We
welcome your comments and suggestions about
People Books. Please write to us at People
Books, Attention: Book Editors, P.O. Box 11016,
Des Moines, IA 50336-1016. If you would like to
order any of our hardcover Collector's Edition
books, please call us at 1-800-327-6388
(Monday through Friday, 7:00 a.m.–8:00 p.m.,
or Saturday, 7:00 a.m.–6:00 p.m. Central Time).